ISBN: 9798323608393
UDC: 930.85; 930.25; 94
DOI: 10.5281/zenodo.105107

CALUSA:
THE LOST TRIBE
OF FLORIDA

(WORLD EVENTS
AND
THE FATE OF THE DISAPPEARED
CIVILIZATION CALUSA AND THEIR
NEIGHBOURS)

KONSTANTIN ASHRAFYAN

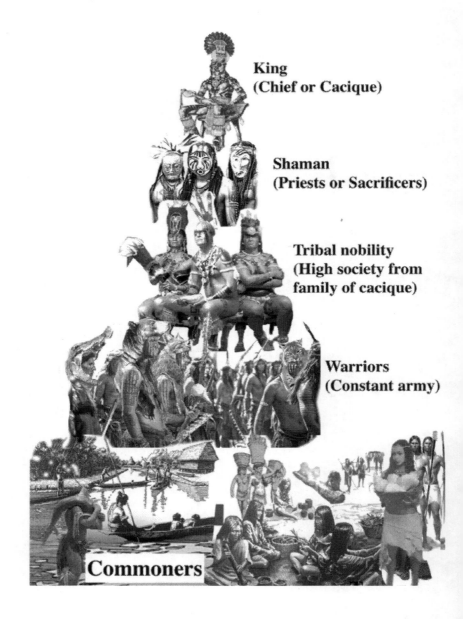

King
(Chief or Cacique)

Shaman
(Priests or Sacrificers)

Tribal nobility
(High society from
family of cacique)

Warriors
(Constant army)

Commoners

CONTENTS

INTRODUCTION
IMPORTANT POINTS FOR UNDERSTANDING THE MONOGRAPH

This work is not intended to be comprehensive or to be an absolute and definitive study. However, despite this, it represents an important valuable insight into the "Pre-Seminole" period in Florida, which few people know about, and which is almost unknown outside the United States.

THE FEW WORDS FROM THE AUTHOR

The purpose of this work is to reveal to the reader the tremendous work done by scientists and enthusiasts, primarily from Florida and America, to revive the **"pages of history torn out by time"** talking about the mysterious people of Calusa. These people have spent their lives trying to restore the history of a forgotten civilization and its secrets. These are heroic people who combine a fiery heart, the will to win and the skills of an investigator who puts together the story of a crime. They have collected tiny fragments of the ruined history of this ancient civilization located on the territory of South Florida. The Calusa society, comparable in its power structure to the civilizations of Mexico and Latin America. Calusa had a unique adaptation to Florida's natural resources. This civilization has been forgotten. But thanks to scientists, enthusiasts, and restorers, we can now see the development and achievements of the people at exhibitions, in drawings, reconstructions, films, games, articles, books and in museums (Appendix 3).

Perhaps someone will also look at us through many centuries and admire us and how we lived with you. But it will be in the future...

In the meantime, let's turn to the past, because studying disappeared cultures and societies helps to better understand the history of mankind and its interaction with the environment and the world around it. The disappeared Calusa tribe from South Florida represented one of the unique cultures – the culture of fishermen-hunter-gatherers (FHG), which has no analogues in history, the study and description of which can provide valuable information not only about its history, social structure, economy and interaction with other tribes and peoples, but also demonstrate unique creativity and diversity, a combination of human capabilities and a favourable natural environment for life and nutrition. By studying the past of Calusa, we can analyse the present and, by analogy with the events of the past, predict the future of many peoples.

It is important to preserve and transmit knowledge about the past, especially about those cultures and societies that have not left their written heritage, as happened with the Calusa tribe, but about which other peoples have records. The disappearance of such tribes and nationalities from the memory of mankind without preserving their history and cultural heritage can lead to the loss of unique knowledge and experience that can be useful to modern societies and understanding of the historical process in world history.

So, on the pages of this book, we will 1) show the development and interaction of the Calusa Indians with other cultures and peoples; 2) show the social structure and organization of the Calusa tribe; 3) consider the economic aspects of life and farming methods, interaction with nature; 4) we will analyse the cultural heritage of the Calusa people, including arts, crafts, mythology and religious beliefs. We will show the influence of the disappeared Calusa tribe and its culture on other cultures and societies, and as a result, conclusions will be drawn about the importance of preserving the history and cultural heritage of the disappeared Calusa tribe for the World History of Mankind.

There are a huge number of stereotypes, misconceptions, myths, and misconceptions about Native American culture based on fiction books, films, and games. For most of the modern population of the earth, the Indians of North America are small primitive communities of aborigines living in simple wigwams and riding horses across the endless prairies in pursuit of bison. And that's all that most ordinary people on different continents know about North American Indians. And it's sad. Few people know that even the horses that the Indians rode were imported from Spain only in the XVI century, and after the destruction of the Spanish settlements spread and multiplied in North America and there are many such myths.

This article presents a different view of the circumstances of the disappearance of the North American Indians of southwestern Florida, the Kalusa tribe and the place of their highly developed society, which "sank forever into the abyss of time", leaving a huge mark on the colonial history of Florida and world North America.

This work is based on the analysis of archival and archaeological materials, as well as the latest data from archaeological excavations. The study examines the peculiarities of the interaction of the disappeared tribe with other cultures and peoples, which makes it possible to determine its unique contribution to the history of the continent, as well as the Bahamas and the Caribbean Islands.

A few words about the terminology used in the work. Researchers of the tribes that inhabited Florida before the arrival of Europeans use different terms to describe the organization of government in the territory occupied by the Calusa people: "kingdom", "state", "weak tributary state" or "complex chiefdom". However, some scientists demand to use the term "weakly hierarchically organized complex state structure" [54] or, as defined by Gailey and Patterson, "a weak state based on tribute" [56, pp. 79-80].

One can argue as much as one like about what is called a "state" [49], but neither in world science nor in international law does there exist a single and universally recognized definition of this concept that would be precisely formulated and reflect all the meanings: spiritual, legal, synchronous, functional, ritual, patriotic, social, demographic, socio-cultural, institutional. But if we consider the state as a political form of organization of society in a certain territory, a sovereign form of government with an apparatus of management and coercion, to which the entire population of the country is subordinated, then the political form of the Calusa people can be completely inscribed in such a framework. the concept of the state. And we urge those scientists who demand a "thorough" explanation of the difference between a "state" and a "weak hierarchically organized complex state structure" not to "rack their brains", since this is not the end of this monograph [10].

We will call the form of Calusa government a "state", understanding and considering that it has specific development features and unique aspects based on internal and external interactions with the environment, tribes, and circumstances affecting it. We agree with all scientists that considering Calusa as a society represents a unique way of a fishing-hunter-gatherer society, and we ask you to consider that we cannot talk about a typical hunter-gatherer tribe or a people whose basis of existence was agriculture [15; 16]. The Calusa did not depend on corn or other crops, and climate and weather changes did not impact the society of this tribe as much as other Indian tribes of the North American continent [110]. Climatic fluctuations were an important reason for the construction of definitely type of buildings, canals which used as the way between villages etc.

In history, there are not many other societies among the aborigines who inhabited North America in the XVI century [17], which are comparable to the Calusa Indians in terms of political complexity and the military alliance they created in southern Florida, which forced the Spanish ships to bypass the peninsula Florida and forget about the Christianisation of this region for 250 long years. Recent discussions in the scientific community, which have not yet been completed, suggest that at various points in the history of Calusa, it can be classified first as a simple chiefdom, then as a complex chiefdom (or supreme chiefdom), and after the 1500s it is possible to talk about Calusa as a "weak state and kingdom, based on tribute" [33].

Nevertheless, we believe that by the middle of the XVI century, the Calusa was a "kingdom" or "very complex chiefdom" of fishermen-hunter-gatherers society with a level of political integration that has no analogy among different societies and non-agricultural societies [59, p. 104-112]; and society Calusa based their power on tribute and marriage unions.

As for the appearance of the Indians of Florida, there is an image that has been ingrained in the minds of many generations of Europe since the end of the XVI century. It started with the engravings of the Dutch-German artist Theodore de Bry, who published a whole series of engravings in his book, published in 1591, intended for the upcoming book fair[1]. The engraver had never been to America, the images of Indians in his books were made in the spirit of the Renaissance and had nothing to do with the real images of the aborigines of the New World.

He himself claimed that his engravings depicting Indians were bought from the widow of an eyewitness to

---

[1] Bry, T. D. Brevis narratio eorum quae in Florida Americae provincia Gallis acciderunt, fecunda in illam Nauigatione, duce Renato de Laudoniere claffis Praefecto: Anno MD LXIIII. : quae est secunda pars Americae. Additae figurae et incolarum eicones ibidem ad vivum expressae, brevis item declaratio religionis, rituum, vivendique ratione ipsorum. Latin language ed., II vols. Frankfort: J. Wechel for T. de Bry & S. Feyrabend, 1591.
URL: https://ia800903.us.archive.org/32/items/brevisnarratio00debry/brevisnarratio00debry_text.pdf or https://archive.org/details/brevisnarratio00debry/page/n101/mode/2up (date of access: 03.03.2024).

the events, the Frenchman Jacques Le Moyne de Morgues, who was a participant in the expeditions of 1562-1665, when the French tried to establish French Florida [114]. But it was a half-truth. De Brie did buy watercolour paintings from the widow of a Frenchman who died in 1588 in England, but how many and which ones are not known[2]? The images of Indians for his books were invented and drawn by the artist-engraver and at the same time by the publisher, most likely himself, because He studied engraving and drawing in the style of the Flemish school. It is in this technique that the "Indians of the New World" are painted. This conclusion can be easily drawn by comparing the technique of De Brie's drawings (Fig. 1A) with the technique of Flemish artists, for example, the famous artist Peter Paul Rubens (Peter Paul Rubens, Pieter Paul, Pieter Pauwel o Petrus Paulus), whose paintings are in the Prado Museum in Madrid (Fig. 1B).

By the way, many watercolour drawings by Jacques La Moyne were found in 1922 in a private collection. Now 59 watercolour drawings are in the Victoria and Albert Museum in London, but they show only the flora of Florida.

The images of Indians invented by De Bry passed from one book to another and formed the images of the

---

[2] Ashrafyan, K. Images of Indians from Spanish Florida in the XVI century: truth and lies, speculation and facts: [report at the meeting The Russian American research nexus 2nd forum (RARN II Forum)] / Konstantin Ashrafyan, PhD History Sciences. 25-27 April 2021.
https://doi.org/10.5281/zenodo.8409846

Indians of Calusa and other peoples of Florida for 500 years. To this day, these images are found in many textbooks and even scientific books and articles.

Only in the XX century in the process of designing museums, reconstructions and exhibitions, scientists together with artists managed to restore real images of Indians [22; 68]. The first to depict the Calusa Indians were the artists who designed the Historical Museum in Tampa Bay, Hillsborough County, Florida (TBHC), Neily and Hermann Trappman[3] (Fig. 2). Especially successful and realistic, in our opinion, are the images of Indians created by anthropologist-illustrator M. Clark[4] (Fig. 3), and the artist T. Morris[5] (Fig.4).

[3] https://tampabayhistorycentre.blogspot.com/2010/07/obscured-by-time-magic-of-florida.html
[4] Clark, M.R., Marquardt, W.H. The Archaeology of Pineland: A Coastal Southwest Florida Site Complex, A.D. 50–1710. Gainesville, 2012. 944 p.
[5] Morris T. Florida's Lost Tribes / with commentary by Jerald T. Milanich. Gainesville, 2004. 70 p.

Fig. 1A. Fragments of engravings by T. De Brie from his book "The Great Journeys", 1591 (left) and fragments of Rubens' painting "The Three Graces" (right)[6]

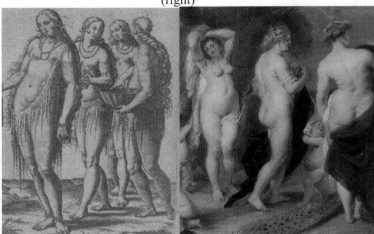

Fig. 1B. Fragments of an engraving by T. De Brie from his book "The Great Journeys" (left), 1591 and a painting by Rubens "The Court of Paris" (right), Prado Museum, Madrid[7]

---

[6] Internet Archive [Электронный ресурс].
URL: https://archive.org/details/brevisnarratio00debry/page/n86/mode/1up?view=theater (date: 03.03.2024).
[7] The Prado Museum in Madrid. URL: https://www.museodelprado.es/en/the-collection/art-work/the-three-graces/145eadd9-0b54-4b2d-affe-09af370b6932

Fig. 2. Artists **Neily and Hermann Trappman**. Photo by Ashrafyan in of the Historical Museum in Tampa Bay, Hillsborough County, Florida.

Fig. 3. *The village of Calusa tribe.* Florida Museum of Natural History in Gainesville, Artist Merald Clark. Photo from Museum by Ashrafyan K.

Fig. 4. The aboriginals of Florida. Artists Theodore Morris. Photo from the theses of Ashrafyan K.

PART I: IN THE FOOTSTEPS OF A VANISHED PEOPLE

PAGES OF SPANISH HISTORY

For the first time we learn about the Calusa tribe from the chronicles of the Spanish conquistadors dating back to the XVI century: from the manuscripts of the Spanish Dominican Bartolome de Las Casas [9], from the chronicles of Antonio de Herrera [45], talking about Juan Ponce de Leon, who officially discovered Florida in 1513 and named this land as *"Pascua Florida"* (or Pascua de Florida) [36; 71] (Fig. 5B, 5C).

There were four women on the list of the expedition team of Juan Ponce de Leon in 1513. Therefore, it can be officially considered that the first women who entered the land of Florida and the present-day United States of America with the expedition of Juan Ponce de Leon were: 1) the Spaniard Juana Ruiz from Jimenez; 2) the maid of Juana Ruiz from Eastern Europe; 3-4) two free black women (it's strange that it's not celebrated in today's Florida - K.A.) (Fig.5A)

After reaching Florida from the eastern part of the peninsula, Ponce de Leon rounded the peninsula and headed to the southwestern part. Until 1519, he believed that he had discovered the island (Fig. 6), where he encountered fierce resistance from the aborigines [36; 85]. Ponce de Leon was unable to land near the modern Estero Bay due to a collision with an unknown tribe (as we now know – with the Calusa tribe). The Indians attacked the Spaniards twice, who had 3 ships and 65 crew members (data on the number vary [36; 71; 85] and are indicated as 49, 54 and 65 people), first for 20 canoes, and the next day for 80 canoes, which could accommodate from several hundred to several thousand people. Neither the cannons on the ships, nor the arquebuses nor the crossbows could help the Spaniards to gain the upper hand [45].

Fig.5A Images of women from the expedition of Juan Ponce de Leon in 1513: the Spaniard Juana Ruiz, her maid from Eastern Europe and two free black women. Create by author by AI (Shedevrum)

Fig.5B. 20-cent commemorative stamp honoring Juan Ponce de Leon was issued on October 12, 1982, in San Juan, Puerto Rico [122; 123].

Fig.5C, The postage stamp commemorating the 500th anniversary of the arrival of Juan Ponce de Leon from Florida, featuring an explorer and a caravel. 2014. The price of the stamp is 0.92 euros [122.123].

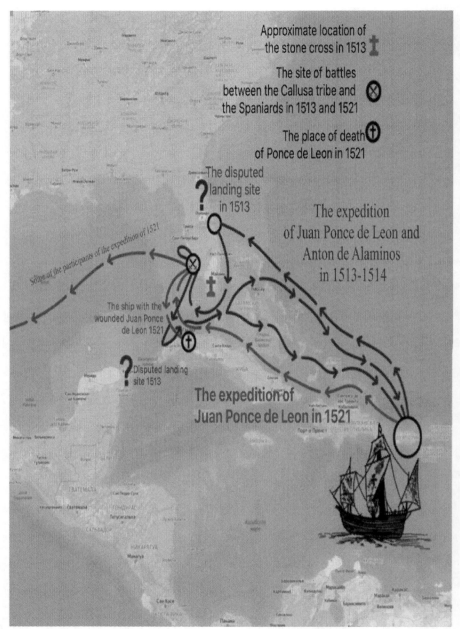

Fig. 6. *The route of Ponce de Leon's expeditions of 1513 and 1521. Drawing by Ashrafyan K.E. on a modern map, edited by Konev S.K.*

Unable to replenish fresh water supplies, Ponce de Leon realized that the expedition could not move north, and had to turn back to the south. Only on the island of Tortuga, where there were many turtles, mammals and birds, the Spaniards were able to replenish their food and fresh water supplies.

We also find a description of the Calusa Indians in the "True Story of the Conquest of New Spain" by the Spaniard Bernard Castillo [3], who witnessed the return of Francisco de Cordoba's ships to Cuba from Yucatan in 1517. The Cordoba expedition accidentally hit the coast of Mexico due to a storm, although the ships were on their way to Florida. Francisco de Cordoba, inspired by the story of Anton de Alaminos about the coast of the peninsula (who in 1513 accompanied Ponce de Leon to the coast of Florida), appointed Alaminos the chief helmsman – navigator of his entire expedition.

On the way back, Alaminos advised Francisco de Cordova to turn the ships towards Florida (Fig. 7A). The Spaniards moored to its western shore, approximately in Estero Bay [38], where Ponce de Leon tried to land in 1513. It was in this place that the Calusa tribe lived. Before they had even landed, the Spaniards were attacked by "tall, strong, dressed in animal skins, with huge bows, sharp arrows and spears in the manner of swords" aborigines [3] (Fig. 7B, 7C).

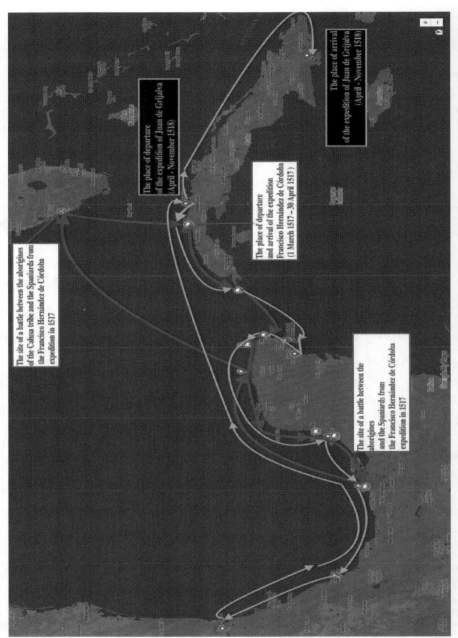

Fig. 7A. *Map of the expeditions of Francisco Hernandez de Cordoba in 1517 and Juan de Grijalva in 1518, which took place with the participation of pilot Anton de Alaminos, who was the chief pilot in the expedition of Ponce de Leon in 1513, drawing on a modern map by Ashrafyan K., edited Konev S.*

Fig. 7B. *The warriors of Calusa, dressed in the skins of a red wolf and a black bear, hold in their hands an atlatl spear thrower, a sword with shark teeth and an axe made of a large shell. The drawing was created by K. E. Ashrafyan.*

Fig. 7C. The author's photo from the original installation of the aborigines of Florida in the Bishop Museum of Science and Nature (ex. Museum de Soto), Bradenton, Florida, USA

The Calusa warriors killed many of the expedition members, mortally wounded Francisco de Cordova himself, and prevented the Spaniards from landing on the coast of southwest Florida and replenishing supplies [109].

New mentions of the Indians of southwest Florida appear in the records of 1521 by Gonzalo Oviedo [69]. In 1521, Juan Ponce de Leon organized a second expedition to establish a colony in southwestern Florida [36]. Landing at approximately the same place where they had first marched – not far from the capital of Calusa Mound Key – the Spaniards founded a fort and a church. The few months that they managed to live in the fort [38] were not calm – Calusa was constantly attacked by aliens, and eventually mortally wounded de Leon and his nephew during another attack [36; 69]. The settlers were forced to leave the fort: one of the ships with the wounded *adelantado* Ponce de Leon returned to Cuba, and the other went to Hernando Cortez in New Spain [114] (Fig. 6).

So, in June 1521, the first attempt of the Spaniards to organize a settlement in Florida ended ingloriously. For almost 250 years, with a short break of 3 years (1566-1569) [114], the Spaniards avoided the southwest and south of the Florida Peninsula.

All subsequent expeditions landed in Tampa Bay, which is located much higher north of Estero Bay and about Pineland (Florida, USA), located in the Pineland

Strait – the main habitat of the Calusa [22]. This bay was a disputed territory between the Calusa tribes and its northern neighbours, the Tocobaga tribes.

An important page in the history of the Florida Indians is the adventures of Alvar Nunez Cabeza de Vaca, a member of the Panfilo de Narvaez expedition. In 1528, Narvaez's land group almost all perished on the coast of Texas. The surviving Cabeza de Vaca spent almost 8 years in various Indian tribes and only in 1536 reached the Spaniards in New Galicia (modern territory in western Mexico). About his wanderings, he wrote the book "Naufragios de Álvar Núñez Cabeza de Vaca"[8], which remains the most valuable information for historians, ethnographers, and other American scientists.

Panfilo de Narvaez was haunted by the treasures discovered by *Cortez* from the *Aztecs (modern Mexico)*, and at the end of 1526, he received a license from the king to conquer and settle the lands of the Gulf coast, located from the Las Palmas River to the Cape of Florida. The license obliged him to go on an expedition within a year, establish 2 settlements, and erect 2 fortresses anywhere along the coast. Together with 600 Spaniards on 5 ships, on June 17, 1527, Narvaez sailed from the Spanish port of *Lucar de Barrameda.* The expedition also included *Alvar Nunez Cabeza de Vaca,* a nobleman from Extremadura,

---

[8] The book "Shipwreck" by Alvarez Nunez Cabeza de Vaca: https://libking.ru/books/nonf-/nonf-biography/1061644-alvar-nunes-kabesa-de-vaka-korablekrusheniya.html#book.

appointed treasurer of the expedition and senior prosecutor (alguacil). Having landed in Tampa Bay in April 1528, Narvaez with 300 Spaniards went deep into the peninsula in search of gold, and the ships went up along the coast, where the groups were supposed to meet. The Narvaez expedition was doomed from the very beginning, because it was based on the incorrect "Map of Garay" compiled by Pineda in 1519, where the distance between Panuco (Mexico) and Florida was only a few tens of kilometres, instead of the real 4,000 km.

We must say that at first, Panfilo thought he was lucky: in one of the Indian settlements, the Spaniards discovered a "golden rattle", and other golden things[9]. Having lost his head from luck, Narvaez began to torture the leader of the Hirrihigua to find out where he got the gold from. The chief refused to give away the secret of the origin of his treasures. And then, enraged by the stubbornness and intractability of the Indian, Narvaez mutilated *Hirrihigua* – and cut off his nose. The news of the cruelty of the aliens quickly spread to all the neighbouring tribes and resulted in a subsequent bloody confrontation all along the Spaniards' path. Narvaez's expedition soured Spanish-Indian relations for decades to come, creating an atmosphere of violence and hatred.

---

[9] The book "Shipwreck" by Alvarez Nunez Cabeza de Vaca: https://libking.ru/books/nonf-/nonf-biography/1061644-alvar-nunes-kabesa-de-vaka-korablekrusheniya.html#book

The ships of Narvaez, who did not wait for the conquistador at the agreed place, returned to Cuba. However, Narvaez's wife demanded that the captain of one of the returning ships go in search of her husband. Coming back to Tampa Bay, the Spaniards landed 4 of their men on the shore, where they allegedly received a message from Narvaez, where they were ambushed. Three Spaniards were killed on the spot, and a young 18-year-old sailor *Juan Ortiz (Sevillian Juan Ortiz)* was captured by the leader of *Hirrihigua*, the one who suffered at the hands of Narvaez and who wanted revenge. The chief prepared a terrible torture for the Spaniard – "barbacoa" [8]. Ortiz was going to be roasted alive over a slow fire, but the daughter of the *Uleleh (or Uleily) Hirrihigua*[10] chief begged her father to spare the life of the white youth. The chief's wife joined in the pleas for clemency, and *Hirrihigua* spared the young Spaniard.

After a couple of years of captivity, Ortiz is supposed to be sacrificed, but again Uleleh (Fig. 8A, B) saves Juan: at night she helps the young man escape to the *Moscoso tribe (or Moçoso)*, where her fiancé was the cacique leader. Upon learning of the Spaniard's escape, *Hirrihigua* became angry with his daughter and

---

[10] Fleming, F. P. The Story of Juan Ortiz and Uleleh // Florida Historical Society. 1908. №1 (2). С. 42–47.; Juan Ortiz and Princess Uleleh Hirrihigua // The New World URL: https://thenewworld.us/juan-ortiz-and-princess-uleleh-hirrihigua/

broke off her engagement. This story became the prototype of the legend of Pocahontas[11].

Juan Ortiz lived for many years with the Moscoso tribe, and thanks to his efforts, the Indians of this tribe forever became allies of the Spaniards. In 1539, Hernando de Soto's men found Juan Ortiz and took him with them [51]. Juan spoke the languages of the *Uzita and Moscoso* tribes (belonging to different groups – *Timucua and Tocobaga*) and helped communicate with the Indians. He told *Hernando De Soto* (Fig. 8 C) a lot of details about the tribes of Florida, including the Calusa, and was the main translator of the Adelantado in his campaign. *Juan Ortiz* died in the winter of 1541-1542, when the expedition was camped in the town of *Autiamke* (modern state Arkansas) [40].

At the time Ortiz was captured, Narvaez's expedition was heading north towards the Apalachee Bay. Imagine the disappointment of the travellers when they realized that this difficult journey was in vain: they did not find any gold and silver, only a lot of corn. The detachment decided to return to the coast and go to the rendezvous point with the ships. Along the way, the Spaniards were constantly attacked by Indians, food was sorely lacking, and many travellers were sick and exhausted (Fig. 8D).

---

[11] The story about the Indian princess Pocahontas, who saved the life of Captain John Smith, and then married the Englishman John Rolfe and became the progenitor of various outstanding families of Virginia, who proudly trace their lineage back to the Indian princess. URL: https://en.wikipedia.org/wiki/Pocahontas

Fig. 8A. Bronze bust of Princess Uleleh или Uleily, who was the prototype of the famous Indian Princess Pocahontas. The bust stood in Tampa until 2018. Photo by K. E. Ashrafyan in 2017.

Fig. 8B. *Memorial plaque about the history of Princess Hirrihigua. Photo by the author. According to updated data, the name of this princess was Ulele (Uleleh или Uleily). Her father's settlement was called Uzita (the big area was Hirrihigua) and belonged to the Tocobaga tribe. Her fiancé's tribe was called* Moçoso *and belonged to the Timucua [41]. Both tribes had different languages [41]. Photo by Ashrafyan K.*

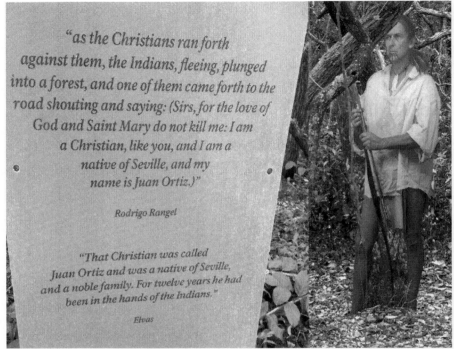

Fig. 8C. Memorial table about Juan Ortiz and installation of image Juan Ortiz from Park de Soto. Florida, USA. The Photo by the author.

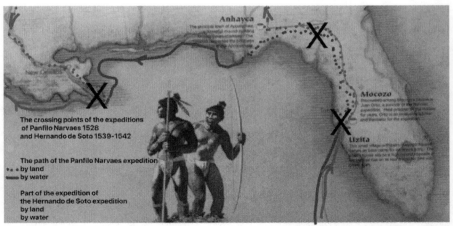

Fig. 8D. The Narvaez Expedition of 1528 and the beginning of the De Soto Expedition of 1539. Map by author

Tired of fighting with the locals, Narvaez decided to sail along the coast of the Gulf of Mexico on boats made from improvised materials. Not far from the delta of the Mississippi River, during a storm, Adelantado and many of his squad drowned – only 80 Spaniards managed to reach the shore, where they were picked up by Indians. Among the survivors was Cabeza de Vaca, who spent 8 years among the Indians, and then wrote a book about Narvaez's expedition, his long return home, as well as about the tribes and peoples he met on his way.

Cabeza de Vaca's book aroused great interest throughout Europe: readers were stunned by the vast territory of Spanish Florida, which stretched from Florida to the North Pole and New Spain (Mexico). Coming from a wealthy family and becoming a famous man who had gained a wealth of experience in his wanderings through the territory that had yet to be mastered, *Cabeza de Vaca* expected to receive the position of adelantado of Florida from the king and engage in the conquest and development of new lands, as he came from a wealthy family and gained a wealth of experience in his wanderings through the territory that had yet to be mastered. However, *conquistador Hernando de Soto* unexpectedly received this position for everyone.

The works of *Garcilaso de la Vega*, talking about the expeditions of *Panfilo de Narvaez* in 1528 and

Hernando de Soto in 1539 to Florida [8; 39], reveal details of the interaction of the Spaniards with the indigenous inhabitants of Florida.

The largest and by far the most famous, thanks to the preserved documents, was the expedition organized by Hernando de Soto, the new governor of Florida and at the same time governor of Cuba (Royal Charter dated May 4, 1537[12]).

On April 6, 1538, the expedition left Spain. It consisted of 9 ships, 230 horses, several dozen dogs (the Indians were most afraid of them), and 20 sows (Fig. 9A).

The expedition consisted of 12 priests who were supposed to conduct divine services among the Spaniards themselves and convert the Indians to Christianity (Fig. 9C).

On May 30, 1539, De Soto landed in Tampa Bay, and on June 3, a ceremony was held to declare the new land a territory belonging to the Spanish crown. The expedition went north from Tampa Bay and was successful, thanks to the freed Juan Ortiz who joined it and became a guide and translator [50].

The expedition lasted for 5 long years – until 1543, ending without Hernando de Soto himself, who died in 1541. The travellers traversed the territory of 11 modern

---

[12] CDI-2, t. 4, p. 431-432; Aleksandrenkov, E`. G. Aborigeny` Bol`shix Antil`skix ostrovov v kolonial`nom obshhestve: Konecz XV – seredina XVI veka. Bel`cy: Parmarium Academic Publishing, 2017. 508 p.

states of America and found traces of the expeditions of Narvaez 1527-1528 and Ayllon 1526-1527 (Fig. 9D).

Fig. 8A. The plaque showing the arrival of the De Soto expedition in 1538. De Soto Nacional Memorial, Bradenton, Florida, USA. Photo by the author.

Fig. 9B. The installation depicting captured Indians during the De Soto expedition. De Soto Nacional Memorial, Bradenton, Florida, USA. Photo by the author.

Fig. 9C monument to the Spaniards and Christian priests who arrived at the landing site of the expedition to convert the local population to Christianity. De Soto Nacional Memorial, Bradenton, Florida, USA. Photo by the author

Fig. 9D. The way of the expedition of Hernando de Soto. De Soto Nacional Memorial, Bradenton, Florida, USA. Photo by the author

This expedition changed the face of the entire territory through which it travelled, bringing with it new diseases, tears, and grief to the local population, which left a heavy imprint on relations between Indians and Spaniards for many decades to come.

Moving north through the Florida peninsula, deep into the continent, de Soto found these lands little attractive, because they deceived his expectations, and there were no treasures there. In addition, the entire tribes showed hostility. The latter circumstance infuriated de Soto, and when he captured the Indians, he showed them special cruelty (Fig. 9B). The commander allowed his men to rape Indian women, rob and burn settlements, and demanded that Christian crosses be installed in their sanctuaries. To protect himself on the way, de Soto practiced taking hostage the leaders of Indian tribes and thus ensured his free passage through the territory.

The Indian settlements visited by de Soto's army were littered with waste from the Spaniards and their livestock, which in a humid climate quickly turned into sources of various pathogenic microbes that were carried by mosquitoes [63].

The news of the merciless Spaniards quickly spread among the Indian tribes over a vast territory and for a long time terrified the aborigines. An example of this is the mention that 60 years after De Soto's death, the Franciscan missionary *Martin Pietro* asked the chief (cacique) in north-central Florida to accept the missionary. The cacique refused, explaining that he had suffered greatly at the hands of Hernando de Soto and his men and would like nothing to do with the Spaniards.

The next mention of the Calusa (although, perhaps, of the Tocobaga tribe, which is the main enemy of the Calusa in the north, near Tampa Bay) occurs after the unsuccessful attempt at peaceful Christianisation of the Indians in 1549.

The Dominican friar *Luis Cáncer de Barbastro (or Luis de Cáncer)* was a proponent of the doctrine of a nonviolent approach to the conversion of American Indians to Christianity, which was professed by the defenders of the Indians Bartolome de Las Casas and Antonio de Montesinos (Fig. 10A). *Luis Cancer* achieved significant missionary success in the Caribbean and Guatemala, after which he proposed to the King to organize a peace mission in Florida. The peninsula has already been ravaged by the expeditions of P. Narvaez and E. de Soto is also very hostile to the Spaniards. Canser argued that further violence would lead the Indians neither to Christianity nor to submission. In 1547, *King Charles* V approved Canser's mission to Florida. According to the royal decree, the monks were allowed to land on the east coast of Florida, avoiding hostile territory in the south and the coasts of the

Gulf of Mexico, where the conquistadors had previously entered.

In 1549, after leaving Veracruz (modern Mexico), Cancer[13], along with his Dominican *brother Fuentes (Lay brother Fuentes)* and the *Fray Diego de Toloza* reached Havana. Then the expedition went to Florida. Despite orders to avoid the Gulf coast, on June 26, 1549, the captain of the caravel landed the missionaries in the Tampa Bay area, just a few miles from the place where previous expeditions landed [38].

This landing led to the martyrdom of 3 Dominican priests in front of the entire crew and showed the impossibility of peaceful Christianisation of the Indians of the southwest of the Florida Peninsula.

This event also destroyed the super-idealistic idea of the "defender of the Indians" Las Casas and his followers about the peaceful dissemination of Christian teachings among the Indians [32]. At the same time, the Spaniards also received important information about the tribes of southwestern Florida from the Spaniard *Juan Munoz*, who spent 10 years (1539-1549) in captivity by the Indians and escaped on a Spanish ship that sailed without the killed Dominicans [89] (Fig. 10B and 10C).

---

[13] Church of St. Louis in Tampa

Fig.10A. Coins with Dominicans - "protectors of the Indians": (above) The coin from the Dominican Republic with a Dominican - Fray Montesinos and other (Montesinos is the first on the coin at the top). The coin from Guatemala depicting the "Protector of the Indians": Bartolomé de Las Casas (Below).

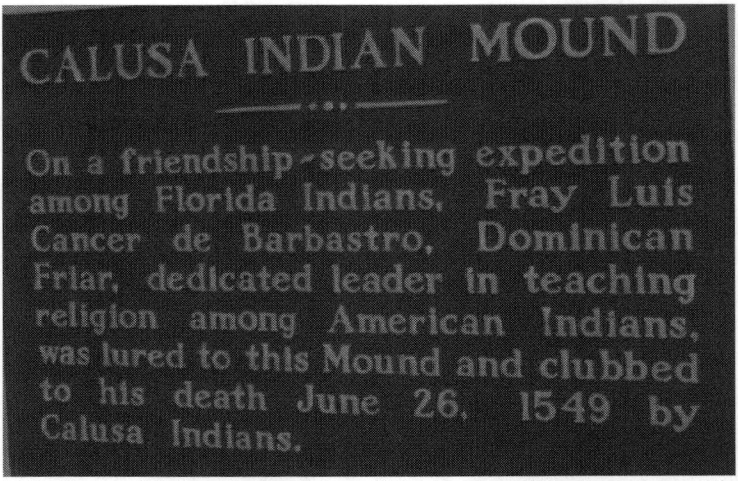

CALUSA INDIAN MOUND

On a friendship-seeking expedition among Florida Indians, Fray Luis Cancer de Barbastro, Dominican Friar, dedicated leader in teaching religion among American Indians, was lured to this Mound and clubbed to his death June 26, 1549 by Calusa Indians.

Fig. 10B. Plaque "Calusa Indian Mound" in the city of St. Petersburg, Pinellas County, Florida. Photo by the author.

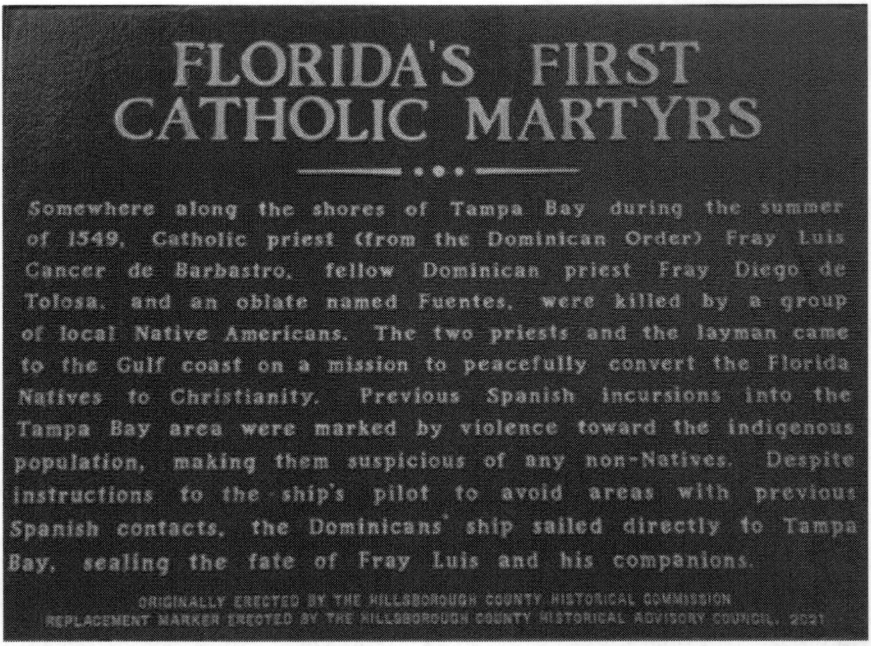

FLORIDA'S FIRST CATHOLIC MARTYRS

Somewhere along the shores of Tampa Bay during the summer of 1549, Catholic priest (from the Dominican Order) Fray Luis Cancer de Barbastro, fellow Dominican priest Fray Diego de Tolosa, and an oblate named Fuentes, were killed by a group of local Native Americans. The two priests and the layman came to the Gulf coast on a mission to peacefully convert the Florida Natives to Christianity. Previous Spanish incursions into the Tampa Bay area were marked by violence toward the indigenous population, making them suspicious of any non-Natives. Despite instructions to the ship's pilot to avoid areas with previous Spanish contacts, the Dominicans' ship sailed directly to Tampa Bay, sealing the fate of Fray Luis and his companions.

ORIGINALLY ERECTED BY THE HILLSBOROUGH COUNTY HISTORICAL COMMISSION
REPLACEMENT MARKER ERECTED BY THE HILLSBOROUGH COUNTY HISTORICAL ADVISORY COUNCIL, 2021

Fig.10C. Plaque in the city of Tampa (Hillsborough County, Florida) in honor of the first Christian martyrs: the Dominicans Father Luis Cancer de Barbastro, Diego de Tolosa and their disciple Fuertes, who were killed by the Indians of southwest Florida in the Tampa Bay area. Photo by the author.

The most important information about the Calusa tribe is contained in the chronicles of *Gonzalo Solís de Merás* in 1566 [64], who was the chronicler of the Adelantado of Florida, who later became governor of Florida and Cuba, *Pedro Menendez de Aviles*. From 1566 to 1568, Adelantado Menendez personally made 4 expeditions to the land of the Calusa people and the king-leader of the Calusa tribe (diff. name Carlos, es. Calos or Carlos) and concluded a friendship agreement with the tribe. Menendez even married the chief's sister, tying himself in kinship with Calusa. His wife converted to Christianity under the name of Dona Antonia. The chronicles of Meras present in detail the way of life and the life of the tribe.

In 1568, Fort San Antonio was built as the capital of the Calusa tribe on the island of Mound Key on the other side of the canal. Soon, the Jesuit fathers Juan Rogel and Francisco de Villarreal arrived there to Christianise the Indians. Rogel left a lot of information about the beliefs and attempts to Christianise the Calusa Indians [106].

In 1566, during the first meeting between Florida Adelantado[14] Menendez and the young cacique chief Caalos (or "King Carlos", or "Rey mayor", or "Great Lord", or "Carlos Zertepe", as the Spaniards called him)

---

[14] Adelantado is the title of a conquistador who was sent by the king to explore and conquer lands beyond the Spanish possessions. This title gave the right to independently organize expeditions without asking for permission from local authorities. The Adelantado could also distribute land and appoint minor officials.

[118] all Christians (6 men and 6 women) were released from captivity, who wanted to leave the tribe (several Spanish women stayed with the Calusa men). Among those released was *Hernando de Escalante de Fontaneda*, who spent 17 years among the Indians of southern Florida (from 1549 to 1566). It was he who became the main translator for the governor of Florida, and after the death of Adelantado in 1572, he recorded memories of the tribes of Florida[15], including the Calusa and their influence on other tribes (Fig. 11A) [97]. His memoirs can be attributed to the main narrative written sources, which have been translated into English (Fig. 11B) and Russian [93; 116; 118]. According to his memoirs, maps of the settlement of various tribes on the peninsula in 1550-1570 were compiled [113; 117; 119] (Fig. 11C).

The Calusa Indians also appear on the pages of books by *Andrés González de Barcia Carballido y Zúñiga*, a Spanish politician, bibliophile, historian of the XVIII century, also known under the pseudonym *Gabriel de Cardenas*, member of the Military Council and the Royal Academy of the Spanish Language, author of the essay "History of I", which He tells about the discoveries and the main events from 1512 to 1722 [98].

---

[15] Fontaneda's recordings have been published under various headings and in different languages: «Fontaneda, d' Escalante. Memoir. Written in about 1575. Translated by Buckingham Smith, with Notes, in Letter of Hernando de Soto», также и «Memoir of Hernando de Escalante Fontaneda. 100 copies, Washington, 1854. Rare. Reprinted, with amended translation and additional notes, 1944, University of Miami and Historical Association of Southern Florida». Перепечатанный в издательстве Glade Publ. Co. в 1945. «Story of his captivity among the Indians of South Florida; a boy of thirteen who was rescued seventeen years later. He was wrecked in 1545».

For almost two centuries after the appearance of white people in I in 1513, the Calusa people fought for their land, their society, and their place in the sun, but lost the battle. The constant wars with the Yamasee and Creek Seminole tribes, who were egged on and supplied with firearms by the British, exhausted Calusa. And in 1711, in the hope of saving the remnants of an ancient tribe, the Spaniards took the last few hundred surviving Calusa to Cuba, to Havana, but in 1762 they fell into the millstones of the war between the British and the Spaniards and disappeared from American history.

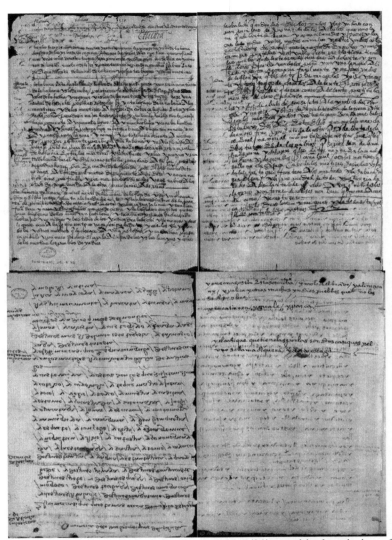

Fig. 11A. Original text by Escalante Fontaneda. Bibliographic description of the document: Archivo General de Indias. [Documento PATRONATO,19,R.32: Relación de todos los caciques de la Florida. [Fecha de creación] 1565, Sevilla] [114].

K. Ashrafyan translated Escalante Fontaneda's texts into Russian and English, although the author believes that Dr. Worth's English translation is more perfect and was done much earlier.

Page 1 and page 2 from the original text while retaining the original titles.

K.E. Ashrafyan's translation of pages 3 and 4 of the original text with an accurate translation of the Cacique enumeration and from other surviving translations in other scientific literature.

The text related to the previous one, on a blank sheet serving as a cover from above, the following was found:

Columbus discovered the islands of Yucayo and Achiti, as well as part of I, along with another neighbouring Santo Domingo.

The Lucayos Islands are of three types, and these are: the first is the Bahama Islands, the second is the Organos Islands, and the third is the Los Martires Islands, bordering some islands of Cape Turtles (Las Tortugas) towards the west (Poniente). These capes are sandy, and they cannot be seen from afar, and for this reason many ships are lost (sinking – K.A.) along the entire coast of the Bahama Canal (la canal de Bahama) and the islands of Tortugas and Los Martires.

Havana (La Habana) is in the south; I (la I) is in the north; and between the land of Havana and the island of Cuba, to Tierra Firme, are these islands of the Bahamas and Organs, the islands of Martyrs and Turtles; they form a channel twenty leagues wide at the narrowest point from Havana to Los Martires and from Martires to Florida, fourteen leagues between the islands in the direction of Spain, more precisely, to the east (Oriente), and through the widest passage to the west goes another forty leagues. There are many shoals and deep channels, but there is no passage for ships or brigs, even if they are smaller, but there is a passage for canoes, and no more, and this is to the east; but through the west, to come to Havana and go to Florida, there is a passage, but not to get to Spain, unless through the main Bahamian Channel between Los Martires and Havana, the islands of Yucayos and Cape Canyaveral (punta del Cañaveral), and it is impossible in any other way. The shortest way to do this would be through the middle of Florida, across the wide river from Tocovaga to the San Mateo River, from west to east, and not by ships, but by land and by water, and some ships would serve others from the same group (in one chain – K.A.) to get to Spain in a different way.

One more memory; I will talk about things in Florida and about the river that flows into the Jordan River, which is on the north side; and we will also talk about the part of the West where Hernando de Soto and Capitán Salinas died, as well as Francisco Francisco de Reinosa and other injured friars and those who were in captivity, some of whom I later saw alive; and we will also show the things, food and clothes of the Appalachian Indians (Abalachi) and Mogoso and other places (tribes?) Below, such as Tocobaga, Osiguevede, Carlos, Ais, Lonsobe and many others, whom I will announce, although not all, and all for this chapter, and first I will talk about the islands of Lucayos and Los Martires.

About the Appalachians, the Indians who walk naked, and about Indian women with bandages made of hay made from trees that are like wool, I will tell you later; and they eat deer, foxes, woolly cows and many other animals; and these Indians collect tribute from low-quality gold mixed with pure, and a lot of coloured skins; and in the river that is in this settlement, there are pearls that they mine, and they are archers, but if the Spaniards attacked them, with a well–informed and skilful translator, they could easily win, and there are no better Indians in Florida than the Indians of Tocobaga, Carlos, Aisa, Tegesta and others, which I will announce further, up to the Jordan River, which I will mention further and tell you about each thing.

The Appalachian Indians are subordinate to the Olagale and Mogoso Indians, as well as other Indians from the lands of the Sierra de Xite (de la sierra de Xite), who are the richest Indians, and these places are considered the most valuable. I spent two years among them in search of low-grade and pure gold, but on the entire coast, which I will later mention in my memoirs, there is neither low–grade nor more or less pure gold, because all they have are ships that have been lost (wrecked – KA), sailing from New Spain (La Nueva España) and Peru (Pirú), they got into a storm in the Strait of the Bahamas, and were found in Cañaveral or Cape Los Martires (Cabo de Los Mártires), which is called Chichijaya, in the direction of the Tortugas Islands bordering Los-Martires and Havana in the south; and the ownership of everything and the essence of everything that lies ahead, I declare, although not in all places, because they have different names that I do not remember, and I stop there.

The land of Appalachia.

Olag [Olagale] (Olagale), Abalachi (Abalachi, i.e. Appalachian), Onogotomo [Onagatano] (Onagatano), Mogoso [Mocoso] o Mocoço, Tocobaga [Tocovaga] (Tocobaga or Tokovaga), Cañogacola o [Cañagacola] (Kangokola o Kanyagakola), Pebe (Pebe), Quega [Esquega] (Eskega), Osigbede [Osiguebede] (Osigbede Osigebede), Piyaya (Piyaya), Tanpacaste (Tanpacaste).

Carlos's land.

Tanpa (Tanpa), Yagua (Yagwa), Tantapaca [Estantapaca] (Estantapaca), Queicher [Queyhcha] (Keicha), Juestocobaga (Huestocobaga), Sinapa (Sinapa), Tomo (Tomo), Cayuca (Cayuca), Neguitun (Nyegitun), Avir (Avir), Cutespa (Kutespa), Çononoguay [Çononogua] (Çononogwa), Quete [Esquete] (Eskete), Tonçobe [Tonsobe] (Tonceobe), Chipi (Chipi), Taguagemue (Tagwahemue), Namuguya (Namuguya), Caragara (Karagara), [Henhenquepa] (Enenkepa), Opacataga (Opacataga), Janar (Hanar), Curu [Escuru] (Escuru), Metamapo (Metamapo), Estame (Estame), Çacaspada (Çacaspada), Satucuava (Satukuava), Juchi (Huchi), Soco (Soko), Vuebe (Vuebe), Teyo (Teyo), Muspa (Muspa), Casitua [Casitoa] (Kasitua or Kasitoa), Cotevo (Kotevo), Coyovia [Coyobea] (Koyobea), Tequemapo (Tequemapo), Jutan o Jutun (Hutan or Hutun), Custevuiya [Custevia o Custebiya] (Custevuia or Kusteviya or Kustebiya).

The Land of Los Martiles [Los Martires]:

Guarungunbe [Guarungube] (Gvarungube or Gvarungunbe),

Cuchyaga [Cuchiyaga] (Kuchiagao or Kuchiyaga), Tatesta (Tatesta), Tegesta [Tequesta] (Tequesta or Tequesta), Tavuaçio [Tavuasia] (Tavuaçio or Tavuasia), Janar (Hanar), Cavista (Cavista), Custegiyo (Custechiyo), Jeaga (Heaga) and Asi (Asi).

The Land of Ice:

Ays (Ice), Vuacata [Guacata] (Vuakata or Gwakata), Tunsa (Tunsa), Mayjuaca [Mayajuaca] (Mayhuaca or Mayahuaca), Maycoya (Maykoya), Mayaca (Mayaka), Çilili (Çilili), Potano (Potano), Moloa (Moloa), Utina (Utina).

Land near St. Augustine

Sotoriba [Sotoriva o Satoriwa] (Sotoriba or Sotoriva), Moloaelbravo (Moloa el bravo), Alimacany [Alimacani] (Alimacani), Palica (Palica), Tacatucuru (Takatukuru), Guale (Gwale), Parca [Paica] (Parka o Paika).

Fig. 11B. The Translation Escalante Fontaneda's texts into English by author.

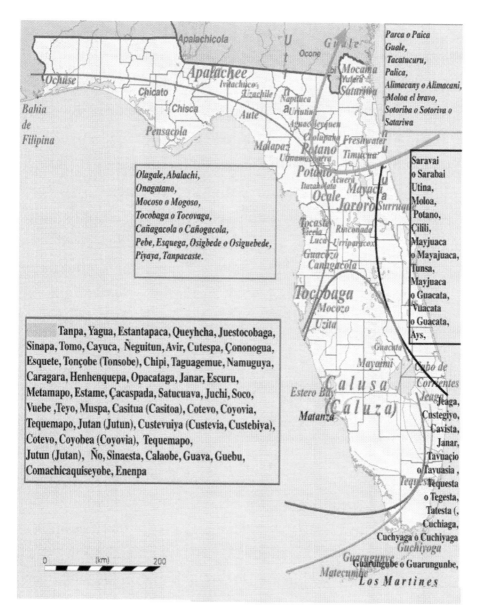

Fig. 11C. The map which based on the text of Escalante Fontana's archival texts from the General Archive of the Indies and other sources (General Archive of the Indies [Documento PATRONATO, 19, R.32: Relación de todos los caciques de la Florida. [Fecha de creación] 1565, Sevilla)] by Ashrafyan K.

COMING OUT OF OBLIVION

The return to the history of the world of the whole people of South Florida began in 1883 when the Simmons couple discovered high clusters of shells at Key Marco, located in Collier County, Florida (Fig. 12) [111].

In 1890, a resident of Mound Key, F. Johnson excavated the mounds, finding artifacts of Native Americans and Europeans – beads and jewellery made of gold and silver, etc. The findings were transferred to the University of Pennsylvania [86]. Then excavations in west Florida were continued by Kenworthy and Douglas who found a system of ancient canals [52; 81]. Wilkinson's excavations followed. Interesting remains near Tarpon Springs (Pinellas County, Florida) were found by Lieutenant Colonel C. D. Dernford, who reported his findings to the rector of the University of Pennsylvania, where the finds from Key Marco had already been found. After resigning from the post of rector in 1894, W. Pepper Jr., MD, together with the American philanthropist, feminist, and suffragist, founder of the Museum of Anthropology F. A. Hearst[16], organized and sponsored an expedition to Florida in 1895-1897 under the auspices of the Bureau of American Ethnology, headed by the famous scientist from the Smithsonian Museum of American Art[17],

[16] Phoebe A. Hearst Museum of Anthropology: [сайт]. URL: https://hearstmuseum.berkeley.edu (date of access: 01.03.2024).
[17] The Smithsonian American Art Museum and its Renwick Gallery: [сайт].
URL: https://americanart.si.edu/ (date of access: 01.03.2024).

anthropologist F. G. Cushing [26; 27; 28]. During the expedition, numerous artifacts were found, currently stored in the Pennsylvania Museum [26]. Cushing concluded that all the findings relate to a phase of some kind of life in South Florida [27; 28]. An important member of the small expedition was the artist V. Savier, who described, photographed, and sketched the artifacts found (Fig. 13), as evidenced by a scientific documentary about the history of excavations in Florida[18].

However, U. Dinwiddie, a member of the Bureau of Ethnology, accused Cushing of forgery of artifacts out of personal hostility and for many years slowed down the research of the disappeared peoples of Florida and the recognition of the discoveries made.

Some places "with very high elevations of shells", which F. Cushing visited in 1895 and 1989 [26; 27], remained intact and became available for research thanks to Don and Pat Randell [22; 28], who in 1994 donated 56 acres of the Pineland (Pine Island in Lee County, Florida, USA) complex to the Florida Museum of Natural History stories for the creation of the Florida Heritage and Environmental Research Centre [22].

---

[18] Domain of the Calusa (https://www.youtube.com/watch?v=u9z9sdokWGQ) – the documentary about the Calusa Indians, filmed in 1995. He introduces a powerful and complex Indian society that new Americans are familiar with, even in Florida

Fig. 12. A photo showing what a cluster of shells in a Mound Whale looked like. Florida Museum of Natural History. Sketches from the 1900 expedition. Photo by K. E. Ashrafyan

Fig. 13 *A.* Key Marco Island, Florida. The place of research of the F. G. Gushing expedition, 1895-1896.

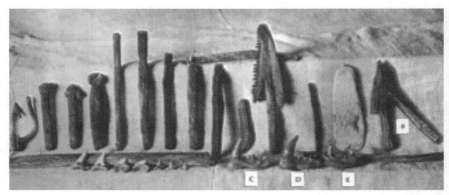

Fig. 13 B. The excavation site of the F. G. Cushing expedition, 1895-1896, and the found tools of labor and hunting. St. Mark's Island, Florida. Photo from the archives of the Pennsylvania Museum

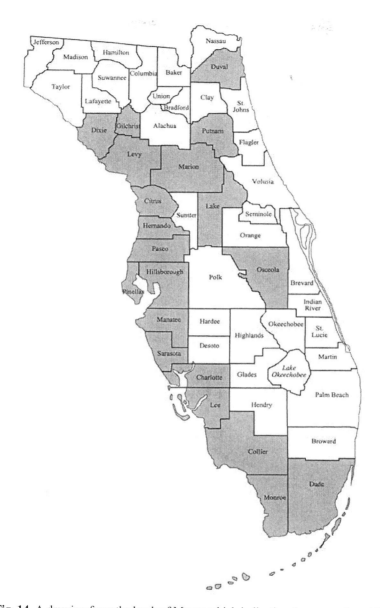

Fig. 14. A drawing from the book of Moore which indicating the areas where his expeditions were excavated, and numerous artifacts were found telling about the life of the tribes of Florida [66].

In the 1900s, archaeologist and writer K. B. Moore conducted multiple excavations throughout West Florida (Fig. 14) [66], also discovering the burial sites of many artifacts from Indian life and European-made goods described by him in his books and articles [67; 79].

D. R. Swanton analysed He made many records and archaeological discoveries and published generalized works and maps about the Indians of Florida and all of North America in 1946 and 1952.[77]

In the first quarter of the XX century, the construction of the strategic highway U.S. Highway 41 began, as a result of which the Florida coastline was destroyed and devastated: many artifacts were lost, shell mounds were destroyed (they were used for construction work and obtaining chalk raw materials) [117].

The main excavation work on the territory of Florida began to be carried out only in the 1970s under the guidance of researcher W.H. Marquardt. With the work of W. Marquardt, who oversees the archaeological and ethnographic collections of South Florida at the Florida Museum of Natural History in Gainesville, a great breakthrough began in the research and popularization of knowledge about the Calusa people. Since 1983 Dr. Marquardt led the Southwest Florida Project, which is dedicated to the found artifacts belonging to the Calusa tribe (present-day Charlotte, Lee, and Collier Counties,

Florida). His numerous writings on the Calusa culture have made invaluable contributions to the study of the Indians of southwest Florida.

Professor D. Hann has written a lot about the interaction between the Calusa people and the Spaniards. His scientific works are devoted to the topic of Spanish Christianisation and its perception by the local tribes of Florida [43].

The works of Professor J. Milanich from the University of Florida are also significant, based on a large archaeological base that allowed us to restore the way of life of the people of southern Florida. As an archaeologist, anthropologist, and curator at the Florida Museum of Natural History, in 2013 he received an award from the Historical Society for his work on restoring Florida's history.

Of particular note is the research of Dr. Worth [90] from the Department of Anthropology and Archaeology at the University of West Florida. His work is very interesting and important and is based on the use of Spanish and other archives. His research has made a huge contribution to the development of historical science and connects the past and present of Florida and its peoples.

Such scientists as Thompson V. D., Thompson A.D., Walker K. J, J. Dietler J. E) made a huge contribution to the fact that the Calusa and other peoples of Florida were brought out of oblivion and took strong positions on the pages of World History - Luer G. M., Lewis C. M., Archibald L. C., Hutchinson D. L., Norr L., Schober T., Marquardt W. H., Walker K. J., Newsom L. A., Scarry C. M., Wheeler R. J. etc.

ABOUT "THE FOUNTAIN OF YOUTH"

MYTH AND TRUTH ABOUT "THE FOUNTAIN OF YOUTH"

I would also like to note one very important moment in the history of the Florida region, which is still poorly sanctified in modern world historical science.

I would also like to mention one very important moment in the history of the Florida region, which is still poorly covered in modern world historical science.

There has always been a boom in searches for the mythical "Fountain of Youth" in Florida. Juan Ponce de Leon allegedly hunted for this echo on the orders of the decrepit monarch and legendary "Catholic king" of Spain Ferdinand II of Aragon, who married an 18-year-old Frenchwoman Germaine de Foix at the age of 54. The "magic water" was needed by the king so that his wife would give birth to the heir of the Trastamara dynasty [112; 121; 122]. And the water had to be located on the territory of modern Florida (Bimini). This myth has developed the Florida tourism industry. And all the owners of 30,000 lakes in Florida claim and prove that it is their lake that is the "Source of youth" (Figs. 15A and 15B).

Douglas Peck, a retired military man, and enthusiast who repeated the route of Juan Ponce de Leon on his yacht [71], proved the inconsistency of this myth: the story of the "Fountain of Youth" in Spanish chronicles and literature was associated with Ponce de Leon by mistake (Fig.16).

Europe learned this legend from the stories of the young Indian *El Chicoran* (baptized *Francisco*), who was captured by the expedition of *Francisco Gordillo* in 1521 [105]. The Indian's story was recorded by the chronicler of the court of Emperor *Charles V, Pietro Martire d'Anghiera* (esp. *Pedro Mártir de Anglería*). The chronicler chronicled the story of the "rich country of Chicora" and linked it with the discovery of Florida by Juan Ponce de Leon, although Gordillo's expedition returned with an Indian prisoner to Hispaniola in In August, from the **Atlantic coast**, but Ponce de Leon's second expedition to the shores of Florida tragically and ingloriously ended two months earlier – in July 1521 and was from the **Gulf of Mexico. However, for the Spanish Chronicler, it connected in one place.**

Further, this story of the "Fountain of Youth" is found in 1535 by Gonzalo Fernandez de Oviedo and is distributed in the works of Lopez de Gomara in 1565, Garcilaso de la Vega in 1580, Antonio de Herrera in 1601. The subsequent fascination with novels and paintings invented on this topic inflated the myth to incredible proportions [105].

Fig. 15A. The sign "Fountain of Youth". The museum and park on the East Atlantic Coast of the USA, St. Augustine, St. Johns County, Florida. Photo by the author.

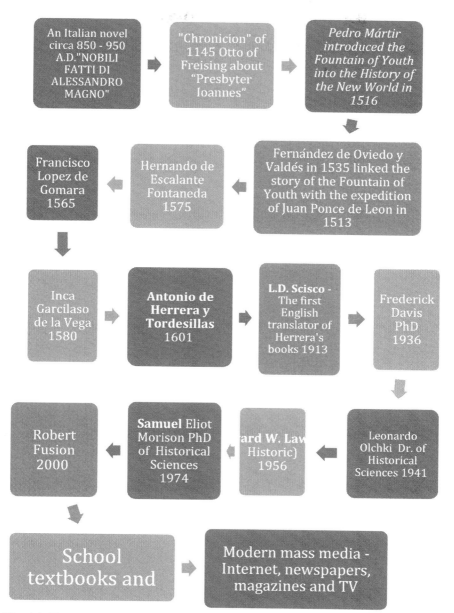

Fig. 16. *The introduction of the myth of the "Fountain of Youth" into the history of the discovery and development of Florida. Correction and explanations to the table by D. Peak made by K. E. Ashrafyan.*

"THE FOUNTAIN OF YOUTH" AND WHO LIVED BEFORE CALUSA TRIBE?

When the first people appeared on the territory of Florida Peninsula in its southwestern part? Who were the predecessors of the Calusa Indians who settled there?

These questions are very relevant.

The above myth of the "Fountain of Youth" led many Floridians to study and search for unusual properties of lakes throughout what is now the state of Florida [112]. After many years of research, as well as studying documents and maps, *J. E. Miller from Washington* decided to check the facts and in February 1942 came to the conclusion that the original *"Fountain of Youth"* was located on the territory of Warm Mineral Springs near the town North Port in Sarasota County, Florida, USA (Fig. 17C, D).

During subsequent searches in the area in the 1950s, Colonel *William Robert Royal* [51], who was an American diver and amateur archaeologist, together with *ichthyologist Eugenia Clark* discovered this unusual lake. The unusual thing was that in the lake at depth there were remains of logs and human bones. The finds were analyzed by radiocarbon dating. And the analysis of the found remains gave a result of 10,000 years, and then at great depths in one of the crevices in this lake a skull with the remains of a human brain was discovered [51; 123].

A big role at this moment was played by the non-recognition and rejection of artifacts found by enthusiasts and amateur archaeologists. These people tried to prove their point of view and presented facts and findings to the court of certified scientists, but the scientific world refused to believe them. Unfortunately, some scientists were limited in their worldview due to the narrowness of the views of other experts of the generally accepted worldview on the settlement of people in Florida. Their opposition slowed down the development of historical science. This happened in the 1950s, when the artifacts obtained in the expeditions were not recognized.

Official science joined underwater research only in 1971-73. Represented by the official underwater archaeologists of the state of Florida - *Wilburn Cockrell*, who were more complacent and supported *Royal*. And at the same time, during the descent into Warm Mineral Springs Lake, other human bones were found, a jawbone and a skull, as well as parts of an atlas that were radiocarbon dated to more than 10,000-12,000 years ago [51].

Official science at that time believed that North America was inhabited only about 3,500 years ago, and Dr. *John Mann Goggin* began to refute these facts and prevented the development of research.

Only many years later, historical science confirmed the settlement of Florida 10,000 years ago (Fig.17A and 17B1).

In 1982, ancient burial sites were discovered in Windover, Brevard County, Florida (Windover Archeological Site, U.S. National Register of Historic Places), on the Atlantic coast of Florida, including 168 remains wrapped in palm leaves and lying-in peat graves (Fig. 17B2). Well-preserved brain tissue was extracted from 91 skulls. The original dating of the graves changed from 500 at the first discovery to 7000 - 8000 BC as an option for further research. Studies have shown that these people belonged to the same people with the common genomes X6 and X7 (The DNA indicated Asian origin, and a relatively rare haplogroup, X.)[19]. Similar burials have been found in other places in Florida and the Gulf of Mexico dating back 5,200 to 12,000 years ago. These people lived up to 60 years old, were tall (175 cm) and ate fish, meat and growing fruits, that is, they were also fishermen-hunter-gatherers. So, Thus, we can talk about the people who preceded the Calusa people who came to Florida as people who came from Asia having a 25% kinship with the Algonquian peoples (Fig. 17B3).

---

[19] The DNA indicated Asian origin, and a relatively rare haplogroup, X. Wentz, Rachel. *Life and Death at Windover*, The Florida Historical Society Press, paperback 2012; URL:
https://myfloridahistory.org/fhspress/publication/life-and-death-windover-excavations-7000-year-old-pond-cemetary

THE QUESTION OF THE EXISTENCE OF THE "FOUNTAIN OF YOUTH" ON THE LAND OF CALUSA TRIBE

Interestingly, it is impossible to completely discard the legend of the existence of magical water on the land of the Florida Indians and the Calusa Indians. The myth of the magical properties of the "Fountain of Youth" is broken down by the facts that are shown in this study. But the legends of the peoples about the source of water, which helps to improve the health of the human body, can still be left. And the fact is that this is confirmed by such science as chemistry and the science of balneotherapy, widespread in Europe. If we stop denying the obvious things, then today scientific evidence confirms the unique chemical composition of the lake *Warm Mineral Springs*, which is located in the *North Port* (Fig. 17C and 17D) [112].

The area of this unique natural mineral spring is 1.4 hectares. The diameter of the lake is 125-175 m, the depth is more than 80 m. The water temperature stays around +30 degrees Celsius all year round, which creates favorable conditions for swimming. The water contains 51 (!) natural minerals (Fig. 17E). Interestingly, the water in the lake changes at different times of the day. Previously, drinking mineral water was even produced on the lake (Fig. 17E). *The Warm Mineral Springs* is currently a unique *balneotherapy* resort in North America and is considered one of the best in America for its properties. From the point of view of the science of balneology, this is an amazing concentration of minerals in the water; after comparison, this gives reason to say that this place is better than the balneological resorts of Baden-Baden and Karlovy Vary in the Czech Republic and the resorts of Hungary. These beneficial properties of the lake have been tested and compared with other *balneotherapy* resorts in Europe personally by the author [112; 121; 122].

A lot of studies of the lake and videos and photographs of the unique lake were made by professional diver Curt Bowen[20].

Florida and USA should be grateful to history lovers and enthusiasts: Director of the Health Foundation, Professor J. E. Miller, Colonel and amateur archaeologist W. R. Royal, ichthyologist E. Clark, diver C. Bowen, D. Peck [71], Ph.D Jeff Merkher[21], G. Gromov, F.G. Cushing and many others [26; 27; 28; 112] who, by their actions, moved historical science forward, despite the initial non-recognition of society.

---

[20] URL: http://www.curtbowen.com/
[21] URL: http://www.jeffmerkher.com/; https://www.chayka.org/node/3931

Fig. 17A. The bust and the plaque erected in Tampa, Hillsborough County, Florida. Photo by Ashrafyan K.

Fig. 17B1. The official information about the history of the area of North Port. Warm Mineral Springs, North Port, Sarasota County. Photo by the author.

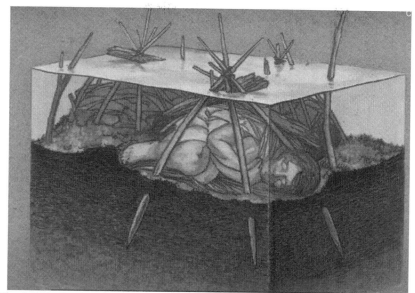

Fig. 17B2. Ancient burial sites were discovered in Windover, Brevard County, Florida[22]

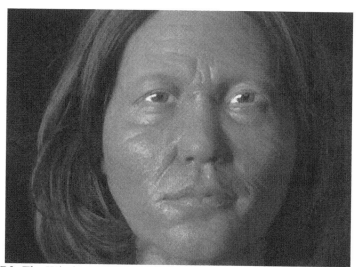

Fig. 17B3. The Windover Woman sculpture by artist Brian Owens, based upon a forensic reconstruction. The sculpture is on display at the Brevard Museum of History and Natural Science[23].

---

[22] URL: https://myfloridahistory.org/frontiers/television/episode/4
[23] URL: https://www.academia.edu/29769805/From_Pond_to_Panels_The_People_of_Windover_Archaeological_Site_Exhibit_at_the_Brevard_Museum_of_History_and_Natural_Science

Fig. 17C. Google Maps showing Warm Mineral Springs from above in the city of North Port, Sarasota County, Florida, USA

The original text

According to authentic historical documents, this warm salt spring is the Fountain of Youth sought by Ponce de Leon. His search for it led to the discovery of Florida on Easter Sunday 1513.

Ponce de Leon first heard of this spring from Indians and one friar Ortiz while he was Governor of Porto Rico. He made a second voyage in 1521 in search of this spring. His ships were anchored at Charlotte Harbor a few miles to the south while on their way here. His party was ambushed by hostile Indians and Ponce de Leon was mortally wounded. He was carried back to this ship and died a short time later.

It is now known that for centuries first Indians and later white men journeyed many miles in search of their health and wellbeing by bathing and drinking these waters.

After many backs of research studying documents and maps in this country and abroad Jonas Miller of Washington d c washable to establish the above facts.

He discovered this spring as the original fountain of youth in February 1942.

Fig. 17D. Warm Mineral Spring, North Port, Sarasota County, Gulf Coast, Florida, USA (Warm Mineral Spring, North Port, Sarasota County, Florida, USA). Photo of memorial plaque by K. E. Ashrafyan

Fig. 17E. Mineral water extracted at depth from water in Warm Mineral Springs. The water contains 51 minerals, and this is indicated on the official packaging. It was also said that you should not consume more than one capsule per day. The bottom of the bottle depicts Juan Ponce de Leon, who allegedly searched for the Fountain of Youth and therefore landed twice in the area of southwestern Florida near this lake. Photo by Ashrafyan K. in 2011

In Soviet, post-Soviet and in the CIS space (the Commonwealth of Independent States), in modern academic CIS space history science the theme about the "pre-Seminole" period in the history of Florida was almost not considered and was dispersed in the first decade of the XXI century. This happened because the main interests of historians and ethnographers have been focused on questions about Russian America in the XVIII-XIX centuries[24] (Fig. 18A) and other tribes and civilizations of South and Central America because Russian science Yu. Knorozov[25] became the founder of the Soviet school of Mayan studies, and due to his identification of the existence of syllabic signs decipherment of the Mayan script, the writing system used by the pre-Columbian Maya civilization of Mesoamerica (Fig. 18B)[26].

The exception is the work of Yu. G. Akimov [1], in which he described the first contacts of the Spaniards with the aborigines of South Florida based on the publications of the enthusiastic researcher D. Peck, who significantly clarified the data on the discovery of Florida and the landing site of the expedition of Juan Ponce de Leon in 1513 [71]. There are many works of A. F. Kofman [4; 5; 7; 8] about the expeditions of the conquistadors to Florida.

---

[24] URL: https://ru.wikipedia.org/wiki/Русская_Америка;
https://en.wikipedia.org/wiki/Russian_colonization_of_North_America#/media/File:Map_of_Russian_America,_1835.gif
[25] URL: https://en.wikipedia.org/wiki/Yuri_Knorozov#cite_note-4
[26] URL: Iurii Valentinovich Knorozov Papers, 1945-1998, MS 2, Image Collections and Fieldwork Archives, Dumbarton Oaks Research Library and Collection, Trustees for Harvard University

Kofman gives a lot of new information from the Spanish archives and mentions the Calusa tribe.

Many publications about tribes of Florida in Internet space were made by *Ignatiy Kostyan*[27]. Tremendous work made creators and editors of the important Internet resource *"The World of Indians"*[28].

The author of this monograph articles has been published about 50 scientific articles in various languages about the Calusa tribe, about expeditions of discovery and exploration of Florida by the Spaniards and the French. Different reports have been presented at various conferences and forums, including and at online meetings of the Academy of Sciences (RAS) in 2019-2020 and at the Russian-American Research Nexus (RARN II) in 2020, where hypotheses were put forward about the development of the tribes of South Florida, their struggle with the Spanish conquistadors, it was told about the introduction of incorrect images of Florida Indians into the minds of Europeans for several centuries. Different texts from Spanish archives were also translated into Russian: documents by Hernando de Escalante Fontaneda [93], appointment documents and reports of Ponce de Leon and other archival materials related to this topic [24; 36; 106]… So, let's set off in the footsteps of the amazing people of Calusa.

---

[27] URL: *https://proza.ru/avtor/cowboy1967.*
[28] URL: *https://www.indiansworld.org*

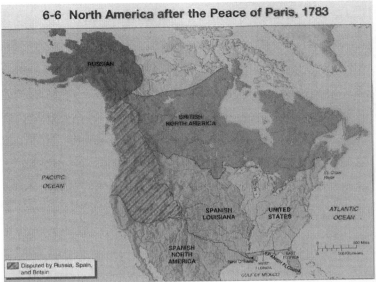

Fig. 18A. The map of the disputed territories in 1783 between Great Britain, Russia, and Spain[29]

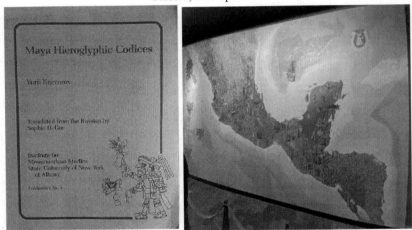

Fig. 18B. The book Yu. Knorozov[30] (left). Map of civilization of Maya, Mexico from Museo Nacional de Antropologia (right). Photo by the author

---

[29] URL: https://www.littlejohnexplorers.com/jeff/revolution/northamericaafterpeaceofparis.jpg
[30]
URL: https://www.amazon.es/s?k=knorozov&__mk_es_ES=ÅMÅŽÕÑ&crid=3CFLQXEH7SILH&sprefix=knorozov%2Caps%2C209&ref=nb_sb_noss

PART II: THE HISTORY OF THE CALUSA TRIBE

WHERE DID THE CALUSA COME FROM?

The self-name of Calusa (/k,'lu:s,/ kə-LOO–sə) means "fierce people", as the Spaniard Escalante de Fontaneda wrote about, who lived among the Indians for 17 years: first with the leader of Calusa Senquene, and then with his successor, Caalos (the Spaniards called the capital of Calusa and its king Carlos, the name of the leader is also found as Kalos or Kaalus). Fontaneda was released only in 1566 after negotiations between Chief Kaalos and Florida Governor Menendez [102; 118].

Europeans called the Calusa tribe in different ways: Calusa, Calusa, Kalos, Calos, Carlos, Kaluus, Caluus, Calculus, Calusa, Caluza) or by the name of the chief – Carlos or Carlos). The Miccosukee Indians called Calusa – Calusashazi (Calushathee), and the Creek Indians – Calushalke (Calushulke), which meant "reapers of the sea", and also perhaps the name was derived from the words Miccosukee – Kalasaali (Calachaalee), meaning "people of shells". For their excellent fishing skills, the Spaniards also called Calusa as "pescadores grandes" (en "great fishermen").

In one of the reports of 1568, there is a designation of the country of Calusa as the country of Escampaba, but it is not necessary to correlate this name with the whole people, this, with high probability, corresponds only to one of the settlements of Calusa and a misinterpretation of the meaning of the word mentioned in the letter of Jesuit Rogel, who did not know the Indian language [106].

The recent generalizing work speaks about the origin and mutual relations of both commercial and cultural between the peoples of the Mississippian culture and the Calusa people. In this work took part such scientists as William H. Marquardt, Karen J. Walker, Victor D. Thompson, Michael Savarese, Amanda D. Roberts Thompson, Lee A. Newsom [57].

In 500 BC, the third wave of tribal migration passed from the Mississippi Valley to the north of Cuba Island through Florida [34; 35; 62]. Many tribes – Alabama, Appalachia, Guale, Illiniwek, Creeks, Caddo, Kanza, Calusa, Mayaimi (Maymi, Maimi), Missouri, Mobiles, Timucua, Cherokee, Yuchi, Yamasee and many others – settled in the south-eastern United States. The Calusa occupied the territory from the southern part of Tampa Bay to Cape Sable and all the islands located in the bays between them.

The researchers suggest that a common religious practice and cultural interaction existed throughout the region. This is evidenced by earthworks and burial accessories.

There was a close trade and cultural connection between the tribes. In mounds and burials throughout the southeast and north of the Ohio River, archaeologists have found many artifacts of non-local origin: alligator teeth from Florida, seashells (especially certain types of molluscs) from the coast and the Gulf of Mexico, etc. [57].

Representatives of these peoples left no written evidence, except for symbols on ceramics, shells, copper, wood, and stone, the artifacts found in mounds and burials. But even these artefacts give an understanding of culture and testify to a complex and not primitive society [20; 21; 33; 62].

In general, all cultures of the post–archaic period of Florida belong to the so-called Mississippian culture – the largest Native American culture that existed in the southeast of America during the VIII-XVI centuries (Fig. 19A), which originated in the Mississippi River Valley and was multinational in its composition. Of the Florida tribes belonging to this culture, the following tribes can be distinguished: Appalachians, Guale, Timucua, Hitchiti, Yamasee, and others, which had the following features:

•   Construction of pyramid mounds with a truncated top, or platform mounds (Fig. 19B).

•   Corn-based agriculture.

• the use of shellfish as an additive to ceramic clay.

• Large-scale intertribal trade.

• The development of the institution of chiefdom, or a multi-level hierarchy of chiefs.

• Centralization of combined political and religious power in the hands of one or more persons.

• The beginnings of a settlement hierarchy, when one large center (with burial mounds) dominated the others.

• A belief system represented by ritual games and a lack of stone architecture.

The peoples living in the vicinity of the Gulf of Mexico practiced seasonal migration: in summer they lived on the coast, using marine mammals, shellfish, and fish in their diet, and in winter they went inland, where they hunted deer, bears, and other animals. Seasonality in foraging was a characteristic feature of many Indian tribes that roamed between areas.

The tribe, which we now know as the Calusa, found a unique place to live in the estuaries of the Gulf of Mexico (Fig. 20). The coast of this region is a very rich estuaries' environment. An extensive network of bays and straits is protected by barrier islands. The Calusahatchi, Myakka and Peace rivers flow into the mouth. There are vast territories of mangroves and seaweed, which ensures high biological productivity.

Black mullet were also found here (Fig. 21) – the only fish that constantly remained in spawning grounds in estuaries [46]. This discovery made it possible for the tribe to lead an all-season sedentary life and develop as a society. The Calusa have remained forever living in the estuaries of Florida.

They developed a complex culture based on estuaries fishing rather than agriculture and created the largest population density and settlements in the region.

The question of how the people who came in the 500s BC and settled in southwestern Florida interacted with the locals who lived before them has not yet been fully studied and does not have an exact answer.

Fig. 19A. The map of the spread of Mississippian culture [31]

[31] URL: https://en.wikipedia.org/wiki/File:Mississippian_cultures_HRoe_2010.jpg (date of access: 03.03.2024).

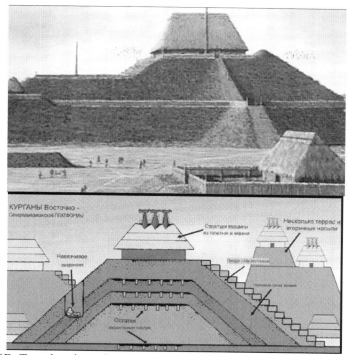

Fig. 19B. Two drawings show the reconstruction of houses located on a hill in Cahokia[32]

Fig.19C. This drawing shows the reconstruction of the Calusa Indians Houses from the Florida Museum in Gainesville.

---

[32] URL:
https://en.wikipedia.org/wiki/Cahokia#/media/File:Mississippian_culture_mound_components_HRoe_2011.jpg

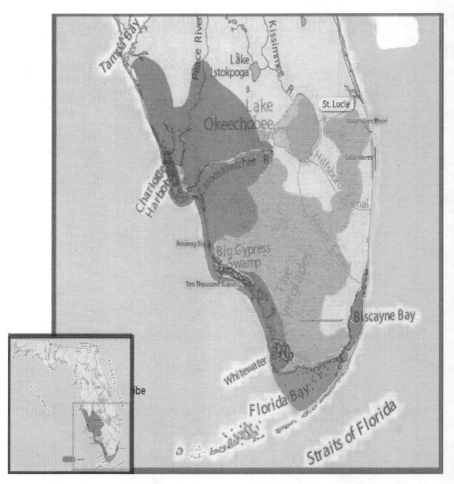

Fig. 20. The map of the probable settlement of the Calusa tribe, based on the formed estuaries of the South Florida ecosystem and the Everglades swamp. Drawing by K. E. Ashrafyan

Fig. 21A. The black mullet (it knows as Loban or mullet-loban (*Latin Mugil cephalus*) is a species of marine ray–finned fish in the mullet family (Mugilidae), the largest of the gray mullets. The maximum body length is 100 cm. It is widespread in tropical, subtropical and moderately warm waters. Valuable commercial fish. In the autumn period, at the end of October-November, the loban enters the brackish water of river mouths, as well as bays and estuaries

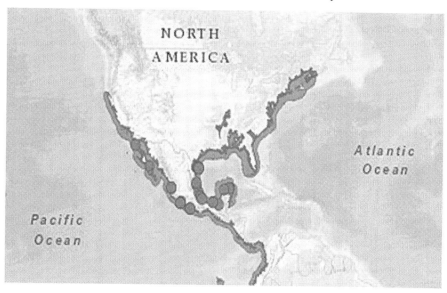

Fig. 21B. The distribution area of Black Mullet in America [33]

Fig. 21A, B. *Black mullet and its distribution area in America*

---

[33] URl: https://www.iucnredlist.org/api/v4/assessments/127923853/distribution_map/jpg (date of access: 03.03.2024).

THE DEVELOPMENT OF THE CALUSA SOCIETY FROM 500 BC TO 1700 AC

Table 1. Periods of development of the Caloosahatchee culture

Cultural period	Climatic periods according by Marquardt	Sea level on the coast of the southwest of Florida
Caloosahatchee I 500 BC – 500 AD	500 BC – 500 AD Roman Warm Period	Low level Sanibel I (500 BC – 100 AD)
		High level Wulfert (100-500 years.)
Caloosahatchee IIA (early) 500-650	Vandal minimum period (Climate change	Low level of Buck Key (500-850)
Caloosahatchee IIA (late) 650-800	caused by cooling and volcanic dust) (500-850)	
Caloosahatchee II B 800-1200	The Medieval warm period (850-1200)	Medieval warm period (Arid for the North America) (850-1200)
Caloosahatchee III 1200-1350	Little Ice Age (1200-1700)	Low cooling period caused by volcanic activity of the Earth (1200-1850)
Caloosahatchee IV 1350-1500		
Caloosahatchee V 1500-1763		

The history of the Calusa people is connected to the Caloosahatchee culture, a type of Mississippian culture that lasted for almost 2,000 years, from 100 BC to 1763. This culture had several periods, influenced by the climate and water levels in the Gulf of Mexico (see Table 1).

The culture and language of the Calusa people presumably originated from the Tunica Indians, belonging to the peoples of the culture of the lower part of the Mississippi River Valley (Fig. 22). The Calusa were linguistically related to the same branch to which the Appalachian and Choctaw Indians belonged, but an unambiguous conclusion on this issue has not yet been made [62; 77].

Representatives of this culture are hunters-gatherers-fishermen who intensively use natural resources. Typical elements of this culture are shell mounds on which the Indians set up their houses, "heaps" of bones and clamshells, tools made of seashells, unadorned ceramic products, as well as a numerous network of water channels that cut the entire country of Calusa.

The economy of Calusa was based on fishing, gathering, and hunting in the estuaries and landscapes of the southwest coast of Florida [63]. The culture of the people did not have a penchant for agriculture or animal husbandry.

Fig. 22. Black mullet and its distribution area in America

Moreover, agriculture was considered a lot of the lower people, and this was an important reason why the Spaniards had nothing to offer for trade and exchange [53]. This is the main difference between Calusa and other peoples of Florida.

In 650-800, the Calusa established beneficial social and trade relations with the tribes who lived in the interior of the peninsula, far from the coast, up to the lake. Okeechobee [60, p. 13-15].

Probably, before 800, the Calusa lived in small formations ruled by Caciques (chiefs) [63, p. 888]. The Indian settlements were small fishing villages, which eventually expanded to the level of large settlements.

Due to the decrease in water in the Gulf of Mexico during the cold period and the reduction in the availability and diversity of fish, the transformation of community life began. Local hierarchical forms of political organization are beginning to unite, which was dictated by the need for families to live together for better household organization in case of food shortages. There is a shift in the type of residential buildings from small houses to larger dwellings where several families can already live [63, p. 878-879]. New types of farming are emerging: The growth of shallow waters allowed Calusa to design dams for growing and storing fish.

At the same time, a highly developed chiefdom was born as a form of government for the tribe. The very identity of the Calusa as a people became possible through the ability to produce and maintain their society through the use of estuaries and surrounding land resources along the southwest coast of Florida. At the same time, the expansion of settlement sites and the creation of economic and political links between settlements, which can be traced through the channels connecting them, continued.

The water channels connecting the coastal towns and islands are rightfully considered a unique engineering structure of the Calusa civilization, especially considering that they were built without shovels (or any metal) and horse-drawn assistance. The Calusa channels, according to scientists, were an important means of communication that helped these Indians develop.

The canal system existed not only on the coast but also in the interior, far from the coastal political centers. The Calusa conducted extensive trade with their neighbors, using rivers and canals as transport arteries.

In the area of 525-675, at the early stage of the Caloosahatchee IIA period, the Calusa inhabited the island of Mound Key [57], which by 1000 became the center of the tribe and began to play a significant role in the region. The geographical location and the construction of the

"King House" contributed to the rise of the city above the rest of the settlements.

A unifying and defensive center always arises at a certain stage in the development of any state. According to the logic of any construction traced in history since ancient times, the town of the king is always a place further away from the enemy, more numerous, more fortified by natural barriers, improved by human hands, as well as with a visible space for early detection of the enemy (high mountains or islands).

Severe storms caused by the onset of the Medieval Warm Period destroyed a third of the barrier islands [76], including Pineland (Fig. 23), where there was a large settlement of the Calusa Indians. The centers of nearby settlements, which previously had influence and political power, cease to be safe and fade into the background [60]. Also, the development of the Mound Key was facilitated by a significant improvement in the shallow estuaries' environment of Estero Bay during the Medieval warm period [79, p. 16]. All these circumstances gave impetus to the development of the island, which was in the center of the bay.

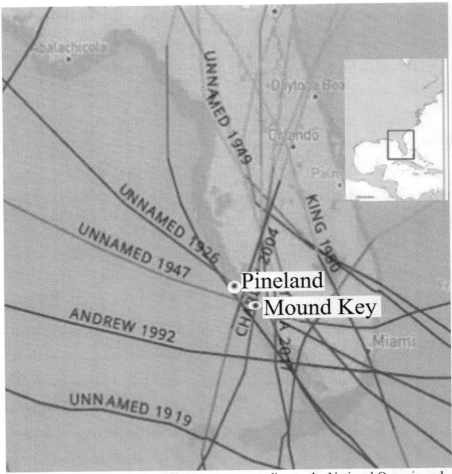

Fig 23. Hurricane paths in different years according to the National Oceanic and Atmospheric Administration (NOAA)[34]

---

[34] URL: https://oceanservice.noaa.gov/news/historical-hurricanes/

In the 900s, the inhabitants of Mound Key began to significantly change the landscape of the island, creating a Grand Canal that divided the island in half and passed between two mounds, 10 and 6 m high [84]. In 995-1030, according to scientists, the construction of the "King House" was started in Mound Key, which was completed around 1045-1140. It was a huge high-rise building capable of accommodating up to 2,000 people, with many rooms and the possibility of holding mass events inside and near the house. The mass nature of rituals and ceremonies emphasized the greatness of the place itself and the status of those people who lived there. Mound Key has become the main place – ceremonial and political – for all the people.

The construction of the "King House" is consistent with the hypothesis that this is due to the transition to a hereditary dynastic form of government within the Calusa people, i.e., the dynasty of rulers who came to power after 950, and the expansion of the boundaries of Calusa influence between 800-1200 [79, p. 16].

Due to the emergence of the "King House" and the emergence of the centre, there was a need to centralize power and redistribute resources to ensure the livelihoods and well-being of community members. The best craftsmen of their craft come and stay in this settlement city, transforming and improving the architecture of the palace; crafts multiply, mass work on building houses, erecting canals, producing canoes, conducting centralized trade with neighbouring tribes, creating a permanent armed detachment of warriors, etc. becomes possible. Public works change the type and way of life, redistributing various types of activities in society [57].

Moral principles in society are also changing: there is a need to act for the benefit of the big house of his tribe. To maintain order, it was necessary to introduce and preserve laws and hierarchy in society, observe traditions, and transfer knowledge from generation to generation [17, p. 10]. Cohesion within the society is growing and hostility with neighbouring tribes is intensifying, which act as external enemies, "cementing" the society of the Calusa people from the inside. The external danger from the surrounding enemies forced Calusa to politically consolidate militarily around the nascent state and its centre, headed by the leader of the entire people.

During the Medieval warm period, between 1000-1075 and 1165-1350, the water level in the Gulf of Mexico was constantly rising. The increased coastal waters expanded the fishing industry of the tribe, which contributed to the growth of trade. For example, shellfish of the *Sinostrofulgur sinistrum*[35] type were valued as a

---

[35] *Sinostrofulgur sinistrum* – съедобный вид крупной хищной морской улитки из семейства Busyconidae, моллюсков busycon. The size of the shell varies from 20 to 45 cm (7.9–17.7 inches). This marine species occurs in the Gulf of Mexico, the Caribbean Sea and the North Atlantic Ocean

material for ceremonial vessels and instruments (Fig. 24), while other types of shellfish were used for pendants and beads [60]. During this period, the fishing-based population of Calusa flourished.

The development of the Calusa society and its way of life has led to the fact that the southwest of the Florida Peninsula is becoming the most populated part with the highest density of settlements and residents them (Fig. 20 and fig. 25).

The rise of Calusa and its position as the tribe-hegemon of the region led to the subordination and conclusion of alliances and treaties with them by other small peoples, who consider external enemies to be a unifying factor and go under the protection of a socially and politically stronger one. This alliance eventually included new tribes and expanded to the south and north. The Calusa began to argue with other tribes for possession of more extensive territories and influence in the region. It is important to note that outwardly the Calusa – tall (180 cm), strong, broad-shouldered - differed sharply from the tribes inhabiting the south and east of the Florida Peninsula and descended from the short natives of the Taino group.

In addition to the hierarchy in the society itself, Calusa had a permanent army. Warriors were separated from fishermen and hunters and no longer participated in foraging or community service but focus on conducting military operations and became the main force in collecting tribute (a similar form of activity was among the vigilantes under the princes during the medieval fragmentation in Russia and knights in feudal Western Europe). According to the description of an eyewitness, the Spaniard Barnard Diaz del Castillo (a participant in the Córdoba's expedition of 1517), the Calusa were "tall, strong, dressed in animal skins, with huge bows, sharp arrows and spears in the manner of swords" [3] (Fig. 26 A, B).

If in the south and east, the spread of influence was not rebuffed, and small tribes submitted to the Calusa, then in the north the Tocobaga Indians and the Timucuan entered into a confrontation with them (Fig. 27).

The Calusa feud with the Tocobaga tribe, who lived around Tampa Bay and north of it, will have a long history. They were different tribes in their culture and these peoples spoke different languages.

Fontaneda noted that the king of Tocobaga was in charge of the Tampa Bay region and "fought with King Carlos" (the supreme ruler of Calusa). According to his statements, the Caciques (chiefs) executive of the Tocobaga and Mocoço settlements were the rulers of "independent kingdoms", and at the time of the first contacts with Europeans, the Tocobaga occupied a dominant position among the chiefdoms of the entire Tampa Bay region.

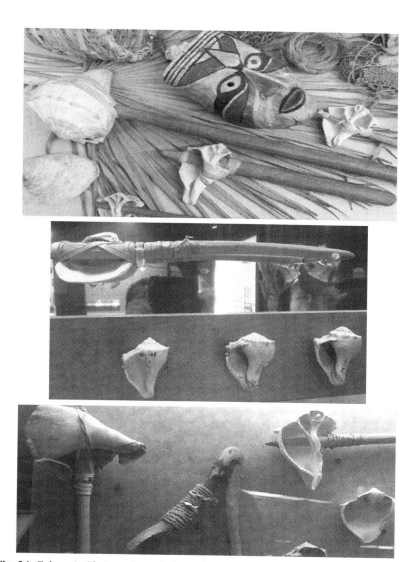

Fig. 24. Calusa Artifacts: axis made from shells of the species Sinostrofulgur sinistrum. Florida Museum of Natural History and other museums of Florida. Photo by the author.

Fig. 25. The territory occupied by the settlements of the Calusa Indians (according to Fontaneda, in 1566 there were about 20,000 people living here in 50 settlements). Drawing by K. E. Ashrafyan

Fig. 26A. The warriors of Calusa, dressed in the skins of a red wolf and a black bear, hold in their hands an atlatl spear thrower, a sword with shark teeth and an axe made of a large shell. The drawing was created by K. E. Ashrafyan

Fig. 26B. The warriors of Calusa tribe, dressed in bear, lynx and alligator skins, hold swords with shark teeth, spears tipped with fish bones, an atlatl spear thrower and axes made from a large shell. The drawing was made by K. E. Ashrafyan by AI Midjourney and Photoshop.

Fig. 27. Settlement of some tribes in Florida. Drawing by K. E. Ashrafyan

The only period that was not so good for the Calusa was between 1025 and 1150. During this time, volcanic activity caused the water level in the bay to drop, leading to a decrease in fish in the bay. As a result, the tribe had to rely more on freshwater fish and animal meat in their diet. But the volcanic eruptions that took place throughout the XIII century. Although they led to a decrease in temperature on Earth [57], they did not particularly affect the people of Calusa, unlike other American cultures.

THE RISE OF THE CALUSA STATE

The discovery of the New World by Christopher Columbus in 1492 and the Spanish exploration of the Caribbean islands that began from that time caused a huge migration process of aborigines from the Antilles and the Bahamas, who fled to the nearest land from them – the Florida Peninsula. Some of them have already been under the rule of the Spaniards and learned the language of the conquerors. Spanish-speaking Indians who fled the Caribbean were present on the side of Calusa in 1513 at negotiations with conquistador Juan Ponce de Leon [36; 58].

By providing the Indian fugitives who arrived from the Antilles and the Bahamas with areas to live on their land, the Calusa naturally received information about the

Spaniards and quickly realized that the "bearded aliens" would soon come to them.

The inevitability of confrontation with a ruthless and superior enemy in all respects pushed the various tribes inhabiting south Florida to forget their grievances and seek an alliance with those who could protect them. In the south of the peninsula, there was only one tribe that was a hegemonic tribe in military, social, and political terms and whose population size and density were much greater than the number of other tribes - and that was the Calusa tribe.

An alliance of Florida Aboriginal tribes was formed around Mound Key, a religious and political centre, to fight against a common external enemy, the Spaniards.

By the beginning of the XVI century, when the Spaniards decided to develop the land north of Cuba, which had no name until 1513 and which was designated as the land of Bimini (Bimini or Beimini), the Calusa people dominated other tribes and had a standing army of well-trained warriors and was also governed through centralized authority with a hereditary leader [58]. The Calusa have come a long way in their development and have become a society that socially represented a vague boundary between a "complex chiefdom", an "archaic state" and the "rudiments of a kingdom" [83].

At the time of the Spaniards' first contact with the indigenous Indian people of Calusa, the latter occupied the territory of southwestern Florida. Geographically, the lands and influence of Calusa extended north from the lands of Tocobaga, Tampa Bay, to the settlement of Santa Elena and Cape Canaveral, and south to Cape Sable, including the Islands of the Martyrs (Los Martinez - the modern archipelago Florida Keys). In addition, the lands of Calusa went to the east, deep into the peninsula, into the freshwater, swampy areas of the lake basin Okeechobee (Fig. 28, 27).

During this period, the heyday of the Calusa tribe, the population was about 20,000 people. The same number of Indians from other tribes lived in the territories under their control [33]. In other words, the Confederacy of the Calusa tribe numbered about 40,000 people. It was the highest population density among the tribes of the Florida Peninsula.

According to the memoirs of Fontaneda [117], who lived for 17 years among Calusa, there were 44 settlements on the territory of the cacique (king) of Calusa tribe (names of places in different languages - Latin and Cyrillic):

1. Tanpa (Танпа)
2. Yagua (Ягва)
3. Estantapaca (Эстантапака)
4. Queyhcha (Кейча)
5. Juestocobaga (Хуэстокобага)
6. Sinapa (Синапа)

7. Tomo (Томо)

8. Cayuca (Кайюка)

9. Ñeguitun (Ньегитун)

10. Avir (Авир)

11. Cutespa (Кутеспа)

12. Çononogua (Çononогва)

13. Esquete (Эскете)

14. Tonçobe o Tonsobe (Тонсобе)

15. Chipi (Чипи)

16. Taguagemue (Тагвахемуэ)

17. Namuguya (Намугуйя)

18. Caragara (Карагара)

19. Henhenquepa (Эненкепа)

20. Opacataga (Опакатага)

21. Janar (Ханар)

22. Escuru (Эскуру)

23. Metamapo (Метамапо)

24. Estame (Эстаме)

25. Çacaspada (Çакаспада)

26. Satucuava (Сатукуава)

27. Juchi (Хучи)

28. Soco (Соко)

29. Vuebe (Вуэбе)

30. Teyo (Тейо)

31. Muspa (Муспа)

32. Casitua o Casitoa

(Каситуа или Каситоа)

33. Cotevo (Котево)

34. Coyobea o Coyovia (Койобеа)

35. Tequemapo (Текемапо)

36. Jutan o Jutun (Хутан или Хутун)

37. Custevuiya o Custevia o Custebiya
 (Кустевуйиа или Кустевия или Кустебийя)

38. Ño (Ньо) (его называли
«любимый город» (pueblo querida)

39. Sinaesta (Синаэста),

40. Calaobe (Калаобе)

41. Guava (Гвава)

42. Guebu (Гебу)

43. Comachicaquiseyobe (Комачикакисейобе)

44. Enenpa (Эненпа)

The preparation of the Calusa for the arrival of Europeans on their lands and the creation of an alliance of tribes dependent on them turned out to be far-sighted and politically literate: they were able to unite the tribes of the south and southwest of Florida and organize well and repel the Spanish invasions in 1513, 1517 and nullify attempts by the Spaniards to establish settlements in 1521 [36, p. 99-176]. Due to the intensity of the shipping lanes between the New and Old World and the growing number of shipwrecks around the Florida Peninsula that could not be avoided, Calusa's wealth grew at an incredible rate, turning it into a powerful authoritarian autocratic state with material symbols of power [83].

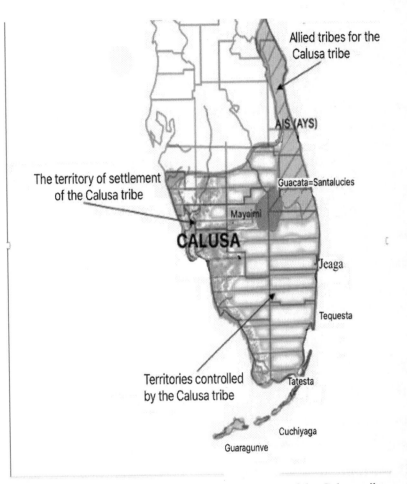

Fig. 28. The zone of settlement and the zone of influence of the Calusa tribe on the modern map of Florida. It was generated by K. E. Ashrafyan

The consolidation of the tribes of southern Florida around Calusa led to the fact that Spanish goods and prisoners captured by various tribes allied with Calusa (Ice, Jeaga, Tequesta, Matecumbe, etc.) or who fell into the hands of Indians in different parts of the peninsula after numerous shipwrecks [65; 90], were delivered to the capital of Mound Key, which quickly This led politically to the autocratic rule of the supreme leader of the Calusa tribe, and therefore the Spaniards correctly called him "king" in their documents [19].

Mound Key, as the "House of the King" of the Calusa people, the centre of the state of the hegemon tribe of the South Florida region, redistributed all captured goods: gold, silver, clothing, European goods, and goods from Mexico, European captives (Spaniards, Portuguese), who became temporary slaves (mostly they were either deprived of their lives on the spot or sacrificed during the holidays) [65]. The captured gold and silver were used by the Indians in jewellery. For example, one of the symbols of royal power in the XVI century was "the decoration of the forehead made of gold and beaded stripes for the legs" [96, p. 310]. The same decorations were distributed to the Caciques of the tribes, symbolizing their sacred affiliation to the alliance with the leader of the Calusa [76], which testified to their political power in the region over other tribes [43].

In order to assert the central authority of the Calusa tribe cantered in Mound-Key and to counteract local elites seeking independence, a permanent army was needed, which the king of Calusa possessed [83, p. 43].

Tributes from other regions and settlements supplied to the capital of Calusa included: food, including bread made from the roots of a plant found around the lake. Okeechobee; mats; animal skins [107]; bird feathers [95 p. 278]; gold, silver, Spanish goods, and prisoners from sunken ships [58]. Local Cacique chiefs in other settlements, both large and small, were responsible for counting and sending surplus products to the capital, regulating production in their settlements, resolving disputes, and coordinating ritual activities in communities while maintaining their duties of subordination to the supreme leader of the Calusa in Mound Key [90].

All the received values and material resources were distributed by the centre among the communities, of which there were about 50 [33].

According to scientists considering the Calusa society [43; 60], with some clarification from the author, the social formation of the tribe during the contact period with the Spaniards was characterized by:

1. A clear administrative, political, cultural, and military centre located in the capital of Mound Key.

2. Administrative and military management from the centre of other large and small settlements of Calusa and territories of allied tribes.

3. Trade in various goods in all directions over long distances, both across the Gulf of Mexico and overland and through the Everglades.

4. The presence of excess product as a result of year-round fishing and fish farming (fishing), regardless of the time of year.

5. The division of the population into conditional estates: higher (Indian nobility, tribal nobility, or aristocracy, or nobility), religious, military, commoners.

6. The sacred status and indisputable authority in religious and political terms of the king of the Calusa people, who has supreme authority over the life and death of his subjects, the hereditary transfer of power of the supreme leader (cacique or king) through the male line (conditionally "Salic form of government with the right of inheritance").

7. The absence of slavery as a driving force in public works: captives (from enemy tribes and Europeans) were either immediately killed or sacrificed to the gods, but they were also allowed to assimilate – marry and have children with other members of the Calusa society [64].

The central authority of the Calusa state was represented by a cacique chief, to whom power was inherited [60]. The king acted as an intermediary between the sacred and secular spheres, led a standing army, and ruled a vast territory with other settlements and allied peoples, as well as within his class society [90, p. 14]. The chief's residence was in the "King House" in Mound Key. His will was fulfilled through the military commander of the standing army. The King and his closest relatives were considered the guardians of religion.

The Indian tribal nobility, or as they say now – high society (aristocracy or nobility in its modern sense) was hereditary. It included all members of the King's family, brothers and sisters, fathers and uncles, and other relatives. The aristocracy expanded due to the birth of children of the tribal nobility or the marriages of someone from the tribal nobility with the leaders of other settlements, other peoples, and tribes. The privileged aristocracy (tribal nobility) did not engage in physical labour [90, p. 43-48]. Representatives of the nobility played the role of "chief Indians" who accompanied the chief during his travels and with whom he consulted on important issues.

To bring together the resources of more remote lands, the king of Calusa needed the help and support of the Cacique chiefs of other lands. The best relations were those based on kinship: each of the leaders gave a daughter or sister in marriage to the king, and from the moment of this union, the enemies of one became the enemies of the other.

The same principle of uniting tribes and expanding their power, as well as subordination to their own interests and the growth of territories through marriage, which was inherent in the monarchies of Europe, was also used by the Calusa. Uniting through marriages, the Calusa state expanded its influence to new areas of land. Marrying women from other tribes helped expand the boundaries of the tribe's influence (both in Europe and Asia). The chief (cacique) and all the tribal nobility (but not ordinary people) had the privilege of having several wives. By the way, Catholic priests opposed this, and it often served as a source of conflict [84].

An important figure in the life of the Calusa people was the chief priest, who was either the retired father of the king of the tribe, or his closest relative. In the religious class, some priests were responsible for the maintenance of temples and idols in them. The priests had a sacred power: they invoked the gods, took care of the dead, keeping in touch with their spirits. Through priests, the Calusa Indians received instructions from the dead [96, p. 279]. The priests were also responsible for predicting bad weather and cataclysms: due to the geographical location of the peninsula, every year, in August-September, the hurricane season hits Florida. Representatives of the cult kept calendars that predicted the weather and had to know herbs, flowers, trees, and their properties, both useful and harmful. Their duties also included holding festivals and religious rituals that supported the power of the leader-king and showed him and his closeness to the gods.

The main force of the cacique leader was the army, which was always headed by a relative of the king. The warriors formed another special group or a separate stratum of society, which was exempt from public works [64; 96, p. 307] and was fully supported by commoners [58, p. 171, 175]. It was a standing army consisting of well–trained, experienced warriors, archers, and those who threw spears with the help of atlatl spear throwers.

The functions assigned to the army were diverse: tax (collecting tribute), police (suppressing uprisings within the state), as well as external military (waging war with external enemies) [49, p. 486]. But the main mission was to fulfill the will of the Cacique king and maintain the mechanism of suppression and control.

The irrepressible Indians terrified all the tribes that inhabited other areas of Florida. The Calusa were rightfully called "cruel people" – their warriors showed no mercy to the enemy. The Cacique chiefs of hostile tribes referred to the Calusa as "fierce warriors" who always achieved what they wanted by force [56].

For the first time in 1513, when faced face to face with the warriors of Calusa, conquistador Juan Ponce de Leon immediately appreciated their military spirit, entering battle with them (Fig. 29).

The commoners are the main and huge stratum of the Calusa society, who were engaged in numerous jobs within the community and in socially useful jobs. These are first-class fishermen who provided food for the entire society (the food of the Calusa people consisted of 80% of the water resources of the Gulf of Mexico), hunters who extract hides and meat, builders of huts, and water channels, those members of the society who cooked food, wove nets, butchered fish and animals, collected edible shellfish, shells and plants, were busy education of children, daily cooking, skinning and sewing clothes, making ropes, nets, baskets, picking berries and fruits and cooking them, etc. (Fig. 30A and 30B).

Over time, a layer of artisans formed in the society, who had skills in the production of pottery, processing of various seashells, wood carving, painting, making religious masks and jewellery made of stone, shark teeth, wood, pearls, and shells; led the production and knew the construction of various types of canoes, cunning devices for hunting, fishing, and war, he planned construction work within the community, laying canals and so on. Other people from the Calusa society had knowledge in navigation and in the treatment of the wounded and sick, and some member of Calusa society traded and communicated with other tribes.

Fig. 29. The attack of the Calusa Indians on the Spaniards. Florida Museum of Natural History. Illustration by M. Clark. Photo from the original by K.E. Ashrafyan.

Fig. 30A. The life of fishermen in the settlement of the Calusa Indians. Florida Museum of Natural History, installation. Photo by K. E. Ashrafyan.

Fig. 30B. The picture of commoners in society of Calusa tribe. The moment of collecting tribute for the leader of the Calusa people. Florida Museum of Natural History. Photo from museum's picture made by K. Ashrafyan.

EXTERNAL AND INTERNAL CAUSAL FACTORS OF THE DECLINE OF THE CIVILIZATION OF THE CALUSA INDIANS (1700-1753)

RELATIONS WITH THE SPANIARDS

From the discovery of Florida in 1513 until 1763, the Spaniards and Calusa entered into peaceful negotiations and political relations several times. The first successful friendly contact between the tribe and the Spaniards was the arrival on the peninsula of Menendez de Aviles in 1566, appointed governor of Florida by decree of Emperor Charles V [18]

Menendez offered Calusa cooperation. The Indians, counting on a military coalition against their enemies, the Tocobaga Indians, went on friendly relations with the Spaniards. First, all the Christian prisoners were released. Then they allowed the Spaniards to build Fort San Antonio de Carlos on the island of Mound Key [82]. A year later, in 1567, representatives of the Jesuit Order arrived in the capital of Calusa to Christianise the aborigines and organized a mission on the territory of the fort [90, p. 31-39, 267-268].

However, the Spaniards wanted peace with all the tribes in Spanish Florida and refused to support Calusa in the fight against the Tocobaga. The Spaniards even tried to reconcile the two tribes. However, Tocobaga was soon taken hostage by a dozen close relatives of King Carlos, including one of his sisters, Dona Antonia, who had already been baptized by the Spaniards [90, p. 261].

The Jesuits, represented by the missionary Rogel, tried many times to Christianise King Calusa and his relatives. However, these attempts provoked a split in society, and the result was a violent change of power of the main leader of the Calusa people. First, the Spaniards killed King Carlos (Caalos). The Christianised Filipe which was the brother of the king of Calusa - Kaalos, was put in place of the main Cacique leader. However, as soon as Filipe began to pursue an independent policy, he was immediately killed by the Spaniards.

The murder of the chiefs, the destruction of the religious centres of Calusa by the Jesuits, and the behaviour of the women of the tribe, who began to cohabit with the Spaniards, embittered the aborigines [119]. Relations with the Spaniards have become a useless burden, binding Calusa, giving them nothing to develop, and aggravating the daily life of the community. All of these led to the action that in 1569 the Indians burned down the capital and left Mound Key. This is consistent with the "Formula of interest" derived by the author earlier in other works (Appendix 2).

Left without material supplies and workers, as well as without the subject of Christianisation, the Spaniards left the fort in the same 1569 and stopped trying to develop southwest Florida for two centuries, stopping only on the Atlantic coast and settling in *St. Augustine* (Fig. 31A and 31B) [84; 90; 114].

It is not known exactly when the Calusa returned to Mound Key, but by the early 1600s, they were again in control of a vast expanse of South Florida [43, p. 9-11].

After 1569 and for the next 100 years, constant hostilities were waged between the Calusa and the Spaniards, as well as other groups of indigenous peoples of Florida who were allied with the Spaniards [90, p. 39-42].

For example, in 1614, the islands of Mound Key and Pineland, with their largest settlements, were the target of Spanish punitive military operations, after the Calusa attacked the Mocoço Indians in 300 canoes. The Mocoço tribe inhabited the eastern part of Tampa Bay between the mouths of the Hillsborough and Alafia rivers (now this place belongs to Hillsborough County) [65] and allied with the Spaniards since the history of Juan Ortiz, who fled to them from the chief Hirrihigua. As a result of a surprise attack by Calusa, 500 Mocoço Indians were killed [60]. The Spaniards avenged their allies and burned Mound Key and Pineland [74, p. 773; 94; 104, p. 773].

In 1679, the Spaniards received information that Calusa was being held captive by several Europeans and demanded tribute from their neighbours [43, p. 23].

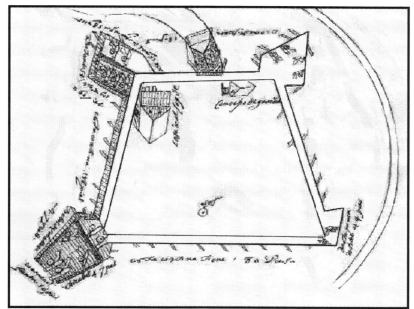

Fig. 31A. *The earliest plan of the Spanish fort of St. Augustine. Main Archive, Seville, Spain*

Fig. 31B. *Reconstruction of the first fort in St. Augustine. Photo by K. Ashrafyan*

Fig. 31A, B. *Fort Sant Augustine.*

In 1680, an expedition left St. Agustin, the main city of the Spaniards in Florida, to free Spanish prisoners [33], which was returned by the coastal Indians of southern Florida, dependent on Calusa, to whom the king of Calusa, on pain of death, forbade the access of foreigners to the territory [43, p. 24-28]. After that, the mission for Christianisation, which was supposed to come to the Calusa chief from Cuba, was cancelled.

The second attempt at peaceful contact between the people of Calusa and the Spaniards took place at the end of the XVII century, when the temperature dropped sharply around the world (the third phase was underway, conditionally XVII – early XIX century., the Little Ice Age) and problems with resources began. Abnormal crop failures and a decrease in fishing were observed (due to the fall of the waters of the Gulf of Mexico) [99]. The standard of living of the people of Florida has deteriorated significantly. Lack of resources, diseases, and constant wars with the Indian tribes allied to the British also exhausted Calusa. From 1566 to 1697 The number of people decreased from 20,000 to about 2,000 people [33]. All these events forced Calusa to move closer to the Spaniards [84].

In 1687, the governor of Spanish Florida, Diego de Quiroga y Lozada, visited the Province of Appalachia to assess the strategic situation. Upon returning to San

Agustin, the governor ordered Captain Primo de Rivera to build a fort[36] on the Chattahoochee River [44], which was supposed to protect the Christianised and loyal Spanish Indians of the Appalachian tribe. The entire province of Appalachia needed protection from the invasions of the Muskogee Creek (Upper Creek) Indians (Fig. 32) and the England, as English traders began to settle and do business with local groups of Creek Indians located north of this Spanish mission[37]. This place was chosen to protect the Appalachians and their main city, Apalachicola.

During this visit, *Governor Diego de Quiroga y Lozada* accidentally met with the son of the king of the Calusa people, who was near *the Appalachian Mountains* and claimed to have been sent by his father to declare his readiness to convert to Catholicism.

In 1689, the Bishop of Cuba, through fishermen, sent an invitation to Calusa to visit the island to establish contact with the king of the tribe. The Calusa chief arrived in Cuba in December 1698, accompanied by some of his relatives, and was baptized [61].

In September 1697, a group of 5 Franciscan missionaries led by *Feliciano Lopez* arrived in Calusa and tried to establish the mission of *San Diego de Compostela*.

---

[36] Fort Apalachicola // Encyclopedia of Alabama: [сайт].
URL: http://www.encyclopediaofalabama.org/article/h-3040?printable=true (date of access: 24.11.2023).
[37] The Chattahoochee Riverbed and the village of Apalachicola were settled by the Muskogee Creek Indians after the extermination of the Appalachian Indians following the massacre by the British and Creek Indians in 1704.

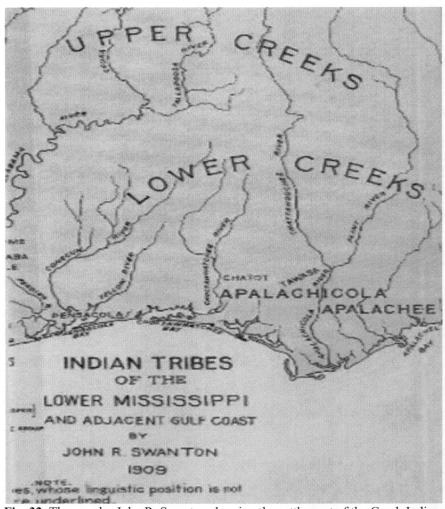

Fig. 32. The map by John R. Swanton showing the settlement of the Creek Indians – Upper Creeks, called Muskogee, and Lower Creeks, called Seminoles. *URL: https://www.academia.edu/40962615/Lessons_from_an_isolate_Chitimacha_diach rony_in_areal_perspective)*

The Calusa expected to receive constant support from the Spaniards in the form of food and gifts for their loyalty. But on December 2 of the same year, without receiving any financial assistance from the missionaries, the Calusa expelled the Franciscans from both the island of Mound Key and their possessions [43].

The Calusa are one of the few indigenous peoples of Florida who have not been Christianized, although history records 2 large-scale attempts by the Franciscans to bring these Indians to Christ: in 1566, when the Spaniards founded the mission of San Antonio de Carlos, and in 1697 when the mission was founded in the lake district. Okeechobee, which lasted only 2 months. The Indians remained faithful to their cultural and spiritual traditions, despite pressure from the Spaniards. "When I went to them to preach Christ, they told me: "What can I give you so that you don't come anymore, go away, we don't want to listen to you," wrote Monk Rogel.

The missionaries noted that the Calusa felt very pain about cutting their hair after they agreed to be baptized. "Losing their hair meant losing their strength, - Fontaneda wrote. – For the most part, they are alien to the perception of Christ, and even those of them who were baptized consider their cacique leaders as confessors and not the monk fathers. When they get sick, they prefer to pray to their idols rather than to God."

All this suggests that for Calusa, respect for nature, belonging to a clan within which their patriarchal way of life was preserved, and they passed on hunting, fishing, gathering, and crafts skills from generation to generation.

EVENTS IN THE NEW WORLD AND THE OLD WORLD. ENGLAND, FRANCE, AND SPAIN

In 1564, the Englishmen visited Fort Carolina in French Florida (near modern St. Augustin, Florida, USA). This happened just a few months before Fort Carolina was destruction by the Spaniards in 1565. After seeing France's successful attempts to establish colonies in the New World in territories that "de jure" belonged to Spain, England decided to explore the New World for herself [50]. The failed British colony in Roanoke in 1585 only temporarily slowed down the plans. But already in 1606, the English King James I gave the task to trading companies to settle the lands of North America between 34° and 45°. In 1607, Virginia was formed – the first colony of the British in North America; in 1620, the Puritans "Founding Fathers" organized the Plymouth colony.

In 1629, King Charles I established the province of Carolina (named after King Charles), which was located "de jure" on the territory of Spanish Florida and included the territory of the current states of Georgia, Tennessee, North Carolina, and South Carolina. In 1660, the monarch Charles II ascended to the throne of England, by his Charter of Carolina order of 1663[38] gave 8 lords from among his cousins and advisers[39] the province of Carolina, and by order of 1665[40] expanded the territories to new borders (Fig. 33).

By that time, it became clear that the creation of colonies was far from a peaceful matter. The Dutch captured the Swedish settlements on the Delaware River and by 1655 expelled them from North America. England in 1664 captured New Amsterdam, founded by the Dutch in 1625, renaming it New York [72]. In other words, two European powers – Sweden and Holland – settled near present-day Charleston. The Spaniards looked at the "Charlestonians" as invaders, and in 1686 the governor of Florida sent an expedition north to explore new lands.

Settlers who came from all over Europe created rice, tobacco, cotton, and other plantations, where African slaves worked (by 1720 they made up most of the American population). However, many more slaves were needed. At the same time, the demand for labour in the West Indies increased sharply due to the export of sugar cane and tobacco from plantations to Europe. Slaves could

---

[38] https://www.landofthebrave.info/charter-of-carolina-words-and-text.htm
[39] Eight lords to whom the English King Charles II allocated lands in America by his charters of 1663 and 1665: Edward Earl of Clarendon, George Duke of Albemarle, William Earl of Craven, John Lord Berkeley, Anthony Lord Ashley, Sir George Carteret, Sir John Colleton, and Sir William Berkely.
[40] https://dn790009.ca.archive.org/0/items/CharterOfCarolina/Charter%20of%20Carolina.pdf

be quickly obtained from the aborigines because black slaves from Africa were very expensive.

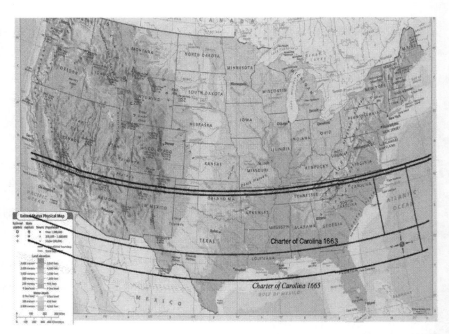

Fig. 33. The territories of North America allocated to colonies by order of King Charles I [i] of England (black lines – borders of 1663; blue color – borders of 1665). The map was compiled by K. E. Ashrafyan

THE SHORT-SIGHTEDNESS OF THE POLITICS OF THE ABORIGINES OF THE EAST OF NORTH AMERICA

The short-sightedness and unwillingness of the aborigines of North America to act as a single monolith against the Europeans led to the almost complete extinction of all indigenous peoples [50]. In their quest for hegemony, they allied with the aliens in the hope that with their help they would gain power over their region and an advantage over other tribes. Winning tactically in the short term, they did not see a deadly future for their people in the long term. Therefore, they were ready to attack their neighbours, mistreat prisoners, and sell them into slavery to whites, receiving weapons, power, and new goods for consumption and trade (Appendix 2).

The war in the New World between the English colonies and Spanish Florida also involved Indian tribes in the confrontation, which became the main supplier of slaves from among the local aborigines. And here the principle of *"Divide and rule"*[41] was fully used by the England (British[42]). The different Indians tribes such as *Westo, Shawnee, Yamasee, and Creeks* who allied with the British were provided with firearms that the Spaniards never gave to the Aboriginal allies.

---

[41] **"Divide et impera"** (Latin)– - **"Divide and rule"** the authorship of this phrase is traditionally attributed to the Italian diplomat Niccolo Machiavelli (XV – XVI centuries).
[42] Kingdom of Great Britain was formed on May 1, 1707 as a result of the signing of the Treaty of Union between the Kingdom of England and the Kingdom of Scotland;; in 1800, the Kingdom of Great Britain and the Kingdom of Ireland united to form the United Kingdom

Since 1702, the tribes of *Miccosukee Creeks*[43] *(Muscogui or Muskoke or Upper Creeks) and Yamasee (Yamassees, Yemasees or Yemassees),* incited by the British, began to make systematic raids into Florida. Their "flying squads" also reached south Florida, the territory where the cities of Calusa were located. The captured Indians were sent by the aliens to northeast Florida, where they were sold into slavery by the British. The tribes of Spanish Florida, who had only bowed and arrows in their arsenal (recall that the Spaniards were against providing guns to the aborigines), proved completely unable to effectively resist the Creek and Yamasee tribes armed with firearms, which the British provided them in abundance.

The number of slaves began to grow at an incredible rate. There were enough of them not only for work inside the colonies but also for smuggling and sale on plantations in the West Indies.

In the XVIII century the Creeks conquered Florida, almost completely destroying the local Indian peoples of Timucua, Miami, Calusa, etc. (the remains were taken by the Spaniards to Cuba) [91].

---

[43] Upper Creeks, called Muskogee, and Lower Creeks, called Seminoles

FRENCH INTERESTS IN FLORIDA

The French colonization of America began in the XVI century and continued until the XVIII century. France established colonial possessions in North America, called New France, stretching from the *Gulf of St. Lawrence* (Quebec) to the *Gulf of Mexico.*

The spread of French influence to North America in the last quarter of the XVII century was helped by: the Governor of New France - *Louis de Buade, comte de Frontenac et de Palluau* and *René-Robert Cavelier, Sieur de La Salle.* During his first term as governor, Frontenac, together with La Salle, founded the lake on the shore. Ontario *Fort Frontenac* to subdue the hostile Iroquois Indians, be able to control the fur trade, and pave the way to the little-explored west of North America. Then they successfully conducted an expedition from north to south along the *Mississippi River,* discovering new lands, which they called *Louisiana* and declaring them a colony of France (Fig. 34A).

The French and English colonists understood that control over the Mississippi River would play an important strategic role in future development and trade, for which each side began to develop a plan to prevent the other from gaining power over these territories. And the *Pierre Le Moyne* brothers played a big role in expanding French influence in this region - *D'Iberville (Pierre Le Moyne, sieur d'Iberville et D'Ardillières) and Jean-Baptiste Le Moyne de Bienville.*

The Spaniards, concerned about French plans to establish forts in the Gulf of Mexico, sent 3 ships with 357 people from Vera Cruz. On November 17, 1698, Spanish ships entered Pensacola Bay (*Bahía Santa María de Galve*) [55]. *Don Andres de Arriola y Guzman* and the Austrian captain-engineer *Jaime Frank* laid the *Fort of San Carlos de Austria* in a place that had already been previously explored by the Spaniards in various expeditions in 1528, 1539, and 1559.

The French, *Pierre D'Iberville (Bienville),* along with his brother and a group of settlers, arrived in the Gulf of Mexico in the same 1698 on 4 ships but were forced to pass *Pensacola Bay*, where the Spaniards were already building a fort, noting the expansion of Spanish Florida to the west.

D'Iberville explored the delta of the Mississippi River and ascended, apparently, to the mouth of the Red River. Finding no convenient place to settle on the river, he decided to establish a colony on the Gulf coast in *Biloxi Bay*, just 100 miles (160.93 km) west of Pensacola. The Spaniards were outraged by the proximity of the French settlement [78].

So, *Fort Maurepas (Fort Maurepas, later Old Biloxi)* was founded – the first permanent settlement of the French in this region. In 1702, the brothers moved the colony to Mobile Bay, located just 50 miles (80.47 km) from Pensacola, and built Fort Louis. Bienville explored the entire region and established trade and friendly relations with local tribes living along the Mississippi River to further cooperate against the British and oust them from the continent.

By that time, English traders from the Carolinas had already established a substantial trading network stretching across the south-eastern part of the continent, which also extended along the entire Mississippi River. The Carolinians, who had little respect for the Spaniards in Florida, were aware of the threat posed by the fact that the French were firmly established on the coast. The governors of Carolina clearly saw the prospects of a possible settlement of the French and Spaniards to the south and west (Fig. 34A).

THE DISAPPEARANCE OF THE CALUSA AND OTHER PEOPLES OF SOUTH FLORIDA IN THE XVIII CENTURY

The disappearance of the Calusa and other peoples of South Florida in the XVIII century.

The final blow to the people of Calusa was inflicted by the "War of the Spanish Succession."

A major European conflict began in 1701 after the death of the last Spanish king of the Habsburg dynasty, Charles II. Charles bequeathed all his possessions to Philip, *Duke of Anjou* (grandson *of Louis XIV of France*), who later became Philip V of Spain. The war began with the attempt of the Holy Roman Emperor Leopold I to defend the right of his dynasty to the Spanish possessions. When Louis XIV began to expand his territories more aggressively, some European powers (mainly England and the Dutch Republic) sided with the Holy Roman Empire to prevent the strengthening of France.

In March 1702, after the death of *King William III* of *England, Anne*, the sister of William's late wife, ascended the throne. On May 4, 1702, Anna, along with Holland and Austria, declared war on the Spanish succession. Other states (Prussia and Portugal) joined the alliance against France and Spain to try to get new territories or protect existing ones.

The war took place not only in Europe, but also in North America. On the American continent, this time, 1702-1713, is known as the "*Queen Anne's War*". In addition to the two main belligerents, numerous Indian tribes were involved in the confrontation. The military actions here were also incited by disputes over the border areas between the colonies of France and England. The most obvious disputes were over the lands along the northern and southwestern borders of the English colonies, which then stretched from the province of Carolina in the south to the province of *Massachusetts Bay* in the north. Settlements in these colonies, some of which were small, were concentrated along the coast, and there were also separate settlements inside the mainland, sometimes reaching the *Appalachian Mountains.*

The interior of the mainland west of the Appalachian Mountains and south of the Great Lakes was poorly explored, inhabited by indigenous tribes of Indians, although French and English traders partially penetrated those territories. The French, who settled at the mouth of the *Mississippi River*, in the town of *Fort Maurepas*, began to lay trade routes further inland, establishing friendly relations with the *Choctaw Indian* tribe, whose blood enemies were the *Chickasaw Indians*, which were allies of the *British*. The French presence in the south threatened the existing trade links that the Carolina colonists had established in the inland territories.

The proximity of the French settlements greatly alarmed the Spaniards, but the Spaniards were even more stressed by the increasingly active actions of the English settlers and their Indian allies from South Carolina. Carolina traders established alliances with the Creek Indians: the Englishmen bought animal skins and slaves captured in Spanish Florida from Indians of allied tribes, and in return supplied the aborigines with firearms.

The territories south of the Savannah River increasingly became the subject of a dispute between the Carolinas and Florida. The conflict was also mixed with hostility on a religious issue between Roman Catholic Spaniards and Protestant Englishmen regarding territories along the coast.

France and Spain joined forces in the fight against the British, although they had recently opposed each other in the Nine Years' War.

In January 1702, even before the official declaration of war, D'Iberville came to the Spaniards with a proposal to act as an armed detachment against the British and their allies together with the Indians of the Appalachian tribe. The British, who learned in advance about the upcoming expedition, organized a defence on the Flint River and defeated a military column led by the Spaniards; at the same time, about 500 Indians who fought on the side of Spain were killed or captured [55].

In May 1702, a military detachment of Creeks, armed and directed by English slave traders, attacked the Spanish mission of the Timucua Indians in *Santa Fe de Toloco* [41]. In the summer of 1702, the governor of San Agustin, José de *Zúñiga y la Cerda* da [55], in retaliation, sent 800 Appalachians to the territory of the Creek Indians, led by *Francisco Romo de Uriza* [72]. By the way, the Spanish attack on the Creek Indians took place not only in 1702 but also earlier - in 1695 – as a reaction to their alliance with the England [91] (Fig. 34A, B).

When the New World received official notification of the outbreak of hostilities, South Carolina Governor James Moore organized and sent armed troops against Spanish Florida.

In October 1702, 500 *British soldiers and militia,* along with 370 *Yamasee Indians*, invaded *San Pedro de Tupico* (Amelia Island, where lived the Guale) on 14 small ships. The British marched along the coast and destroyed the Christian mission of *San Juan del Puerto* along with Catholic Indians from among the Guale and Mocama. When the British entered St. Agustin [72], the city was empty - all the inhabitants took refuge in the fortress of Castillo de San Marcos. Moore did not have powerful artillery to destroy fortifications. After 7 weeks of the siege, 2 Spanish warships arrived at the fortress, sent to help from Havana, and the British had to retreat [30]. But before that, they set fire to the residential areas of San Agustin.

The campaign was a disaster for Moore. Considerable funds were spent on its organization. In addition, the expedition disgraced the colony's authorities in front of the mother country and the Indian allies.

Therefore, upon his return to Carolina, Moore resigned as governor and decided to restore his reputation on his own.

The Spanish population of Florida at that time was quite small compared to the population of the nearby English colonies. Since its foundation in the XVI century, the Spaniards have created a network of missions, the main purpose of which was to pacify the local Indian population and convert it to Roman Catholicism. In the province of Appalachia (approximately in the territory of modern west Florida and southwestern Georgia) there were 14 missionary communities with a total population of about 8,000 people in 1680. Many of these communities were inhabited by the Appalachians and other tribes who migrated to the area.

After Moore's expedition destroyed coastal towns in Guale Province, Florida *Governor Jose de Zuniga y la Cerda* ordered the remaining Spanish missions in Appalachia and *Timucua Province* to be combined for defensive purposes. The missions in *Mocama Province* were consolidated south of the *St. Johns River*, and the missions in Timucua were consolidated in San Francisco de Potano.

The Indians of Florida, who had neither firearms nor help from the Spaniards, became the easiest and simplest target of the tribes engaged in the slave trade. The Spanish policy of not giving firearms to the natives, even to the allies, was a tragic mistake by Spain.

In early 1703, the Creeks attacked the missions of *San Jose de Ocuya* and *San Francisco de Potano*. As a result of these raids, up to 500 Indians were enslaved (Fig. 35).

All these raids showed the insecurity and weakness of the Spaniards who occupied Spanish Florida.

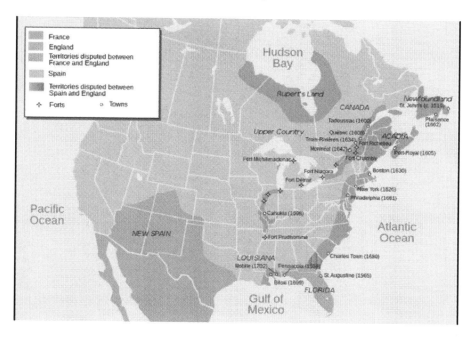

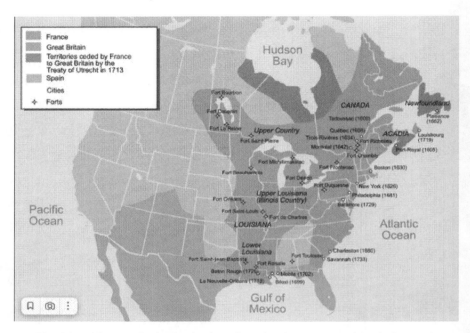

Fig. 34A. Changes in the territories of England, France, and Spain in North America during the War of Anne II from 1702 to 1713 and in the next 100 years

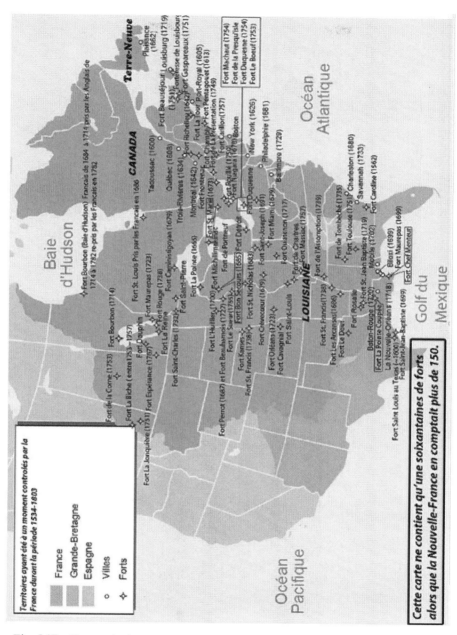

Fig. 34B. Changes in the territories of England, France, and Spain in North America during the War of Anne II from 1702 to 1713 and in the next 100 years – until 1804, when all of Louisiana was sold by France to the United States.

Fig, 35A. An attack by Creek and Yamasee Indians armed with firearms on the Calusa settlement. Florida Museum of Natural History. Illustration by M. Clark

Fig. 35B. Seminole Indians attack the Calusa Indian village. The drawing was created by the author based on photographs from the Museum of Seminole Indians Ah-Ta-Thi-Ki, and his own drawings, and his own drawings, as well as a drawing from AI (Shedevrum)

Shortly after his resignation, James Moore presented the Carolina authorities with a plan for a new expedition to Florida, which he intended to finance at his own expense. Despite the recent setback, the new governor of Carolina supported Moore and even helped him by appealing to allied Indian tribes to take part in the campaign.

On January 25, 1704, Moore, along with 1,500 Creek Indians and Yamasee, went to one of the largest Catholic missions in Florida - *Ayubala,* in the province of *Appalachia (Apalachicola Province).* While most of his forces were destroying the surrounding villages, the ex-governor of Carolina himself attacked the settlement at the mission. *Priest Angel de Miranda* hid people in a local church and organized its defence. 26 men, protecting their wives and children, shot back at the British for 9 hours [30]. When the ammunition ran out, Miranda entered negotiations with Moore and agreed to surrender. After the besieged, including 58 women and children, left the walls of the church, they were all brutally murdered, and the mission burned down.

Word of the attack on Ayubale reached San Luis de Appalachia, 24 miles to the south, where *Captain Juan Ruiz de Mejia* gathered a force of 400 Appalachians and 30 Spanish cavalrymen. However, the arriving detachment was defeated by the superior forces of the Carolinians. More than 200 Appalachians and more than a dozen

Spaniards were killed or captured, including *Captain Mejia*. For the Spaniards (8 prisoners) Moore wanted a ransom.

After the Battle of Ayubale, Moore continued his march through the Appalachian Mountains. In the expedition report, Moore claimed to have killed more than 1,100 men, women, and children. He also stated that he "sent into exile" 300 and "enslaved" more than 4,300 people, mostly women and children [55].

This raid went down in history as the "Appalachian Massacre." The British and their Indian allies destroyed 13 Spanish missions, which were never rebuilt [72]. The Appalachians were once a powerful Native American nation allied with the Spaniards in the region. However, the surviving and demoralized Indians no longer believed in the ability of the Spaniards to protect them and, for the sake of saving their lives, began to side with the British.

In the following years, the Carolina settlers and tribes allied to the British conducted an unhindered slave hunt, almost destroying the indigenous population of Florida (including the Calusa people) [72]. The destruction of Appalachia and the absence of regular Spanish troops in Florida (except for San Agustin) became a verdict for the peoples of Florida and the Spaniards themselves (Fig. 36).

In the following years, British colonists continued to raid Spanish and French interests in Florida and the Gulf coast, but they failed to capture St. Louis, San Agustin, Pensacola, and Mobile, the main settlements of Spain and France.

In 1706, the Spanish expeditionary force under the command of French officer Francois-*Louis D'essonville de Maneval* and Spanish General *Juan Andres de Pez*, with the support of Indian allies, launched a second invasion of South Carolina. South Carolina Governor *Nathaniel Joseph* successfully organized the defence of Charleston and repelled the Spanish-French invasion [72].

In the period from 1670 to 1715, from 24,000 to 51,000 aborigines were exported through the ports of the English colony of Carolina [34], of which more than half (from 15,000 to 30,000) were brought from Spanish Florida [37].

By 1710, the settlements of Calusa Mound Key, Key Marco, Pineland, and dozens of others were burned and destroyed by the Creek and Yamasee Indians, the inhabitants were killed or taken into slavery to the British (Fig. 35 A, B).

In 1711, the Spaniards evacuated 270 Indians, including Calusa, to Cuba and placed them in the east of Havana, where 200 of them soon died [119]. Nevertheless, there were still about 1,700 aborigines in Florida, whom the warlike tribes methodically pushed to the south of the peninsula in the Florida Keys [43, p. 418-431; 92]. The deserted territories of the once powerful Calusa tribe were occupied by the Creeks and related Seminole Indians who came here (Fig. 37).

In 1763 Spain ceded Florida to England. The remaining Calusa were resettled by the Spaniards to Cuba, where they completely disappeared among the population. But in Cuba, the last Calusa was overtaken by fate – the war came to this region as well. It was in the place where the last representatives of the once powerful tribe were settled that the fiercest battles between the Spaniards and the British were fought.

Having disappeared from history, Calusa still managed to leave its mark: the place where the remnants of the tribe lived in Cuba after 1763 became the centre of fishing. And who but *"Pescadores Grandes"* could share the secrets of fishing with Cuban fishermen [25; 75].

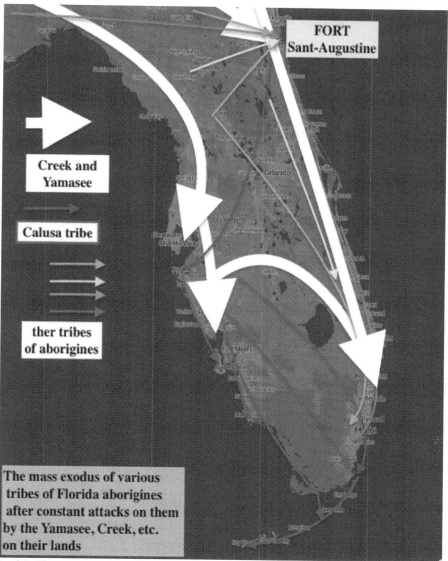

Fig. 36. The mass exodus of various tribes of Florida aborigines from their land after constant attacks on them by the Yamasee, Creek, etc. on their lands. Drawing by K. E. Ashrafyan

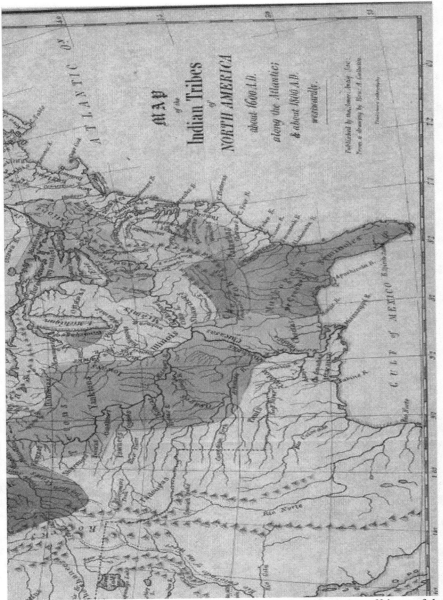

Fig. 37. A map showing the settlement of the Seminole Indians (an offshoot of the Creek Indians) in the devastated territories previously occupied by the Calusa and other tribes. *URL: http://www.virginiaplaces.org/nativeamerican/cherokee.html*

PART III. THE WAY OF LIFE OF THE PEOPLE OF CALUSA TRIBE

We learn about the way of life, habits, religious traditions, technical achievements, and hierarchy of the Calusa tribe from the surviving records of eyewitnesses of the events – Hernando de Escalante Fontaneda and chronicler Solis de Meras, captives of the tribe who had to learn the Indian language, observe alien customs and norms of behaviour adopted by local residents. Recall that the sources of the Calusa script have not been found, and therefore the details of the life of this people have been known to us only since the XVI century, with the arrival of the Spaniards in Florida.

POLITICAL ORGANIZATION OF THE SOCIETY

The Spaniards, having gotten acquainted with Calusa, noted the complexity of the political organization of their society, which was divided into classes. By the XV–XVI centuries, the following pyramid of power was formed (Fig. 38):

1. The Supreme Leader (King) of Calusa is the absolute secular and religious ruler of the entire nation.

2. Indian nobility – the chiefs (Caciques) of other settlements who had blood ties with each other through the marriage system and were the agents of the policy of the supreme leader.

3. The caste of priests (shamans) is spiritual leaders who supported the traditions created by society through worship of the gods and rituals aimed at deifying the supreme ruler, the inviolability of the foundations, and the divine election of the nobility.

4. The permanent army is a stratum of society that was engaged in collecting tribute, suppressing uprisings, waging wars, and did not take part in public works.

5. Commoners (fishermen, hunters, artisans, builders, gatherers, etc.) – members of the society on which the entire state of Calusa was based (it is known from the records of the Spaniards that commoners did not work hard all day – they had enough time for rest, religious rituals, and creativity).

Each city was ruled by a chief (cacique). The leaders of the Calusa tribe, unlike other cultures, inherited their power within the kindred clan from which they came. The ruling clan, as a rule, was the "supplier of personnel" for the entire management system. The cities of Calusa were administratively represented by chiefdoms. One chiefdom could include from one to several cities. According to Fontaneda, in 1570 there were about 50 chiefdoms in the "state" of Calusa.

The country of Calusa was ruled by the supreme leader (king), who had absolute power over all chiefdoms.

Fig. 38. The Pyramid of the Calusa Society [44]. Create by Ashrafyan K.

[44] Ashrafyan K. E. The hypothesis of the inevitability of the failure of attempts to develop the south of the Florida Peninsula from 1513 to 1525 (Chapter 8.) //Science, education, society in the context of digitalization: monograph / Under the general editorship of G. Y. Gulyaev. Penza: International Centre for Scientific Cooperation "Science and Education", 2021. pp. 143-156.

During receptions, he sat in a special place (a kind of stool on the platform), which emphasized his superiority. An important place, but with a rank lower than the supreme ruler of the Calusa people, was occupied by a military leader and a high priest, whose power was also unlimited and extended to the entire territory of Calusa (Fig. 39).

Spanish sources from 1564 indicate that the supreme leader, the military leader, and the high priest were closely related to each other. The priest was the king's father, and the war chief was his brother. The power of King Calusa was also inherited from father to son, but there were exceptions. The Spaniards pointed out that if the king did not have a son, then he was obliged to marry his sister, who had a son, in order to transfer power over the country of Calusa to him.

Spanish sources from 1564 indicate that the supreme leader, the military leader, and the high priest were closely related to each other. The priest was the king's father, and the war chief was his brother. The power of King Calusa was also inherited from father to son, but there were exceptions. The Spaniards pointed out that if the king did not have a son, then he was obliged to marry his sister, who had a son, in order to transfer power over the country of Calusa to him.

The King of Calusa tribe and the Indian nobility had the right to have several wives and marry several times women not from his clan, as well as from friendly or allied tribes. Such marriages were concluded to create the necessary political union. In addition, there was a custom when the supreme ruler married the sister, daughter, or spouse of a tribal leader defeated during the war, this indicated the surrender of the loser and his unquestioning submission to the power of the winner.

The authority and right of the clan to govern society were obviously based on the legends of the clan's origins. Of course, the Caciques and the nobility came from these noble families, as it was and is all over the world even now (the royal dynasties of Europe and Asia).

The members of the clan aspired to power and from time to time disputed the right to inherit the "throne". An example of the struggle for succession can be seen in the history documented by the Spaniards during the reign of Menendez (1565-1572).

The king of the Calusa – *Senquene (Senkwene or Senkene)*, who ruled at the beginning of the XVI century and did a lot to unite the peoples of southern Florida, had no male heirs [56]. The *chief priest (main shaman of Calusa tribe)*, who was the chief's brother, also had no sons. Then Senquene "adopted" the son of his wife's brother (brother-in-law's son), who is known to the Spaniards as *Felipe*, so that he would become his successor.

Fig. 39A. The Chief Cacique (King) Calos (or Carlos) of the Calusa tribe.
Reconstruction, Florida Museum of Natural History. Photo by K. E. Ashrafyan

B. The War Chief   **C.** The High Priest

Fig. 39B, C. *Representatives of the tribal nobility (aristocracy) of Calusa. Reconstruction, Florida Museum of Natural History. Photo by K. E. Ashrafyan*

Fig. 39D. Representatives of the tribal nobility (aristocracy) of the Calusa tribe – on the left is the young wife, and on the right is the old wife of Carlos. *Reconstruction, Florida Museum of Natural History. Photo by K. E. Ashrafyan*

In 1534, a marriage was concluded between the 10-year-old Filipe and the 4–year–old daughter of Senquene, Antonia.

Senquene went to the spirit world when Filipe was still young and could not rule the state. After the death of the supreme leader, the father of Filipe and the chief priest (Senquene's brother) decide to rule together until Felipe comes of age. At this time, the chief priest finally gave birth to a son, who was named *Kaal (or Calos, or Kaalus, or Carlos - K.A.)*.

The chief priest forces the widow Senquene to annul the marriage of her daughter *Antonia* to *Felipe,* and then arranges the marriage of the old widow queen with her young son Kaal, putting him in line to rule. To calm Felipe's father, the boy is appointed the new military commander. Felipe marries for the second time, this time to the daughter of the chief priest [59, p. 180-184]. These events caused discontent among many Calusa, who perceived it as a usurpation.

King Calusa - Kaalus (Carlos) probably took over the royal post in the 1550s, because it was with him that Pedro Menendez de Aviles met in 1566. Carlos's succession was not well-liked by the Caciques of other powerful chiefdoms. In 1556 in *Okatchaqua*, the chief of the Cape Canaveral - Ice tribe, sent his daughter to Mound Key to marry her to King

Carlos. But on the way, cacique *Serrop* intercepted her and married her himself, thereby challenging the authority of the supreme cacique and disrupting the key alliance and trade route between Calusa and Ice.

RELIGIOUS TRADITIONS

The best means of political persuasion for Calusa was religion. The Calusa had a complex worldview system based on the worship of the forces of nature and ancestral spirits. The main objects of religious worship were 3 deities. Each deity fulfilled his role: the most powerful ruled the physical world and the change of seasons, the second controlled the rulers of the Calusa people, and the third helped in the war (Fig. 40A, B).

Calusa believed that each person has 3 essences, or 3 souls: one lived in his shadow, the other soul was in his reflection and the third soul was in the pupil of the eye (Fig. 41).

After a person died, the soul of the pupil joined the souls of the dead, with whom the living could talk and consult. The other two migrated into other substances – inferior, compared to the human body, for example, into some animal, and after its death into a fish, and so on, until the soul disappeared completely [95, p. 279]. The soul could leave the body during a person's life, and to find it and bring it back, the help of a healer was needed: outside the temple, a priest lit a fire to help a lost soul find its way into its human body.

The Trinity, the same as in many religions of the world, adapted to way of life of the Calusa people and contributed to the consolidation of society through a common and understandable faith.

The priests used wooden masks during the ceremonies, which were hung on the walls of the sanctuary after the ceremonies (Fig. 42). Carved masks made of wood were an integral part of religious rituals. Fontaneda noted that "the priests in witchcraft masks with horns looked like devils who, during ritual orgies, ran around the city and howled like dogs at the moon and the stars." These products revealed the artistic and spiritual value of the Calusa culture. "A primitive artist, – noted the archaeologist F. Cushing, who created these masterpieces, was probably a man with refined taste because the painting and carving with amazing precision and delicacy convey the mood and desire of the one who wore these masks".

Calusa, according to scientists from Florida, confirming the words of Spanish eyewitnesses and reports of monks from different orders, had a lot of time for singing, dancing and what we can now call self-development.

In the 1930s, folklorist, anthropologist and ethnographer at the Smithsonian Institution *Frances*

Densmore collected Seminole songs (Low Creek) and together with them learned about the songs of the Calusa people. Some songs of the Calusa Indians were heard from the Seminoles and were recorded by her in a musical version - for example, "*Songs from the Hunting Dance*" and "The Song of the Corn Dance" (Fig. 43).

The description of the annual sacred ritual of experiencing death and rebirth has been preserved [58]. The ritual lasted 3 days. Six armed men, belted with ropes, danced, and shouted, shaking rattles, around a 2.5-meter-high wooden blockhead with a high vertical pole with a wide arrow instead of a head. The pole, like the dancers, was painted red and black. The men danced in a frenzied rhythm until they were exhausted.

Fig. 40A. The three deities of the Calusa people. Florida Museum of Natural History, illustrated by M. Clark. Photo from the original picture made by K.E. Ashrafyan.

Fig. 40B. The gods and deities of Calusa. Florida Museum of Natural History, photo from the original, author Ashrafyan K.E.

Fig. 41. The existence **of three souls in the human body** according to the beliefs of the Calusa tribe. Drawing and created by K. E. Ashrafyan and AI Midjourney

Fig. 42A. *Calusa masks. Florida Museum of Natural History. Photos from originals and compilation by K. E. Ashrafyan*

Fig. 42B. Shamans of the Kalusa tribe wearing masks during a religious ceremony. Created by Ashrafian K.

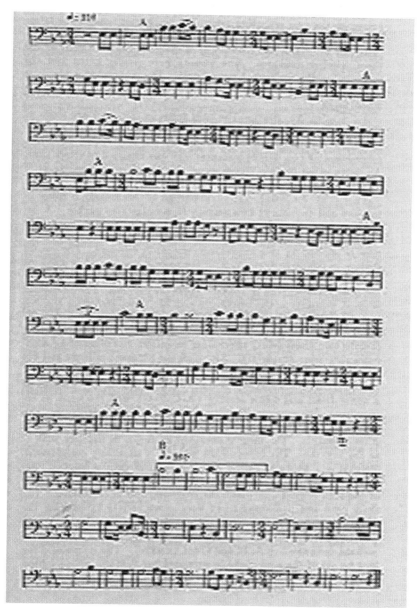

Fig. 43. Notes from the book «Seminole music». №25 «Calusa Corn Dance Song»[45]

[45] Densmore, Frances Seminole music. Bureau of American Ethnology. Bulletin 161. Plate 1 изд. Washington: Goverment printed office, 1956. p.61.
URL: https://archive.org/details/seminolemusic0000fran/page/n61/mode/2up

Then they reinforced their strength with cassina berries and a "*black drink*" (Fig. 44) and continued the dance [47]. Exhaustion and ingestion of *Cassina berries* and a "*black drink*" containing coffee stimulants caused mental hallucinations and led to a variety of experiences and inappropriate behaviour that can be observed in modern drug addicts [18].

Human sacrifice was an important part of the religious life of Calusa. Foreigners were sacrificed to the idols of Calusa, as well as Europeans captured after shipwrecks. Sacrifices were considered gestures to propitiate spirits, as well as ways to gain favour from the forces of nature [90]. "*To smash the head with a club to a warrior who fell asleep on duty, or to chop off the head of a prisoner is a common practice for them...* - Fontaneda wrote. – They do all this to satisfy their idols. They oblige every tribesman to sacrifice human flesh to an idol at least once in his life" [102].

By sacrificing Christian captives, the kings of Calusa and religious leaders emphasized the insignificance of the faith of their enemies and showed the exaltation of their idols, against which sacrifices were made. The ceremonies were supposed to show the population the mortality of previously unseen "bearded aliens." The chronicler of Menendez, who was in Mound Key in 1566, wrote that in the settlement they were met by "about 50 Christian heads mounted on stakes on a fence" [42].

One of the elements of Calusa's religious beliefs was the belief that their supreme ruler was able to see and communicate with the world of invisible spirits. If the cacique could not enter into a trance and communicate with spirits, then society distrusted him, and his power was in great question.

Caciques were essentially not only administrators but also clerics. They had the power to grant or take the lives of their subjects at their discretion. For the people not to lose faith in their ruler, the priesthood, military leaders, and, in general, the entire Indian nobility used the religious beliefs of the population to preserve in society the value system on which the power of the cacique and the structure of society has been held for centuries, in fact, as in any country in the world to this day.

The religion of the Calusa with their human sacrifices, veneration of ancestors, deification of the king, and unconditional submission to his will lead to a complete consolidation of society, in which life for the sake of society was higher than the life of everyone. It is important to note that the Calusa treated the elderly with respect and this was different from many other Indian tribes, where the attitude towards the elderly was negative or even contemptuous.

Fig. 44A. *Ilex Cassine* или *yaupon holly leaves*, It grows throughout the Florida Peninsula

g. 44B. *Ilex Vomitoria*, it grows only in the central and northern parts of Florida

The "black drink" of the Florida Indians

The black drink played an important role in the rituals of the indigenous peoples of Florida and the south-eastern United States and was a decoction made from the leaves of various types of holly growing in Florida:

1) tea holly (*Ilex vomitoria*);

2) Japanese holly (*Ilex cassina* or *yaupon holly leaves*).

An analysis of the methylxanthine content in the leaves showed that if we take 100% of the caffeine content in tea holly, then Japanese holly contains only about 20% caffeine compared to it (Arabica coffee beans contain only 8% caffeine).

Making a drink:

1. The leaves were dried in ceramic dishes over an open fire (i.e., fried, similar to coffee beans).

2. After roasting, the leaves were brewed in boiling water, which contributed to the rapid dissolution of caffeine (caffeine dissolves many times faster in boiling water). The colour of the broth turned out to be black, hence the name – "black drink".

3. The broth was poured into ritual dishes.

4. They consumed the drink in a warm form.

A certain type of large shells was used as tableware for the drink.

This energy drink was consumed ritually, and its physiological hallucinogenic effects were based on its high caffeine content.

Fig. 44C. Fruits of plants for the "black drink" of the Florida Indians and its ingredients

EXPERIENCED SAILORS AND TRADERS

Life on the seacoast, estuaries, and mangrove forests of the Gulf of Mexico made the Calusa skilled sea hunters and seafarers. The main channel connecting Calusa with the sea was considered the mouth of the Caloosahatchee River, from where the Indians went far out to sea in canoes - dugout boats - to trade on islands located nearby and even far from Florida. Calusa boats also sailed along the west coast, engaged in fishing, lifting cargo from the bottom of the sea from the wrecked Spanish ships, some of which the Indians then skilfully used in trade, exchanging with neighbouring tribes.

Calusa canoes had excellent seaworthiness. Intricately designed, with elongated bows, the 15-foot (about 5 m) boats were carved from single cypress or pine trunks. The Indians soaked a hollow log with resin and set it on fire, after which they scraped out the core with special cutters made from seashells.

The researchers noted that the Calusa canoe's draft was only a few inches, allowing the boats to navigate easily through shallow waters and swampy mangroves. The oldest Calusa canoe was found in 1956 in the swamps of South Florida. According to the results of radiocarbon analysis, its age was about 5000 years (Fig. 45).

It is known that there were several types of canoes in Calusa: a rough water canoe and a quiet water canoe. There was a type boat as catamaran: its were made from two canoes connected by poles with a platform fixed between them were also used, on which goods, cargo, or important persons (chiefs, Indian nobility or priests) were placed. The warriors of Calusa tribe used the same type when attacking the Spaniards (Fig. 46). Calusa's catamarans went on long trips across the sea (Gulf of Mexico, Atlantic Ocean) and lake Okeechobee. Calusa set sails on the canoe that were made from finely tanned animal skins. The chronicler of Governor Menendez noted that the Calusa Indians were well oriented by the North Star when guiding the governor's ships at night and accompanying their chief Carlos in a canoe in 1566.

The Calusa, whose settlements were located at the southern tip of the peninsula, as well as on the islands of the Gulf of Mexico, in the period 1150–1550 were actively trading. Their boats regularly sailed to Cuba [98], they knew about the existence of advanced civilizations in Yucatan, with whom they maintained trade relations [60]. Contacts between the Calusa and the Maya are evidenced by numerous artifacts, most notably the design of the Calusa canoes for sea travel, which identifies them with Maya boats [71].

The Calusa tribe traded with other tribes and peoples living along the Mississippi River, along the Gulf of Mexico, on the Atlantic coast, and in the Caribbean.

According to the view of several scientists, it was determined that Calusa spread the trade connection due to not only by the need to purchase some goods, but also by the very significance of this process, during which social relations were formed.

An important element of the Calusa's policy and trade policy was the marriages of their caciques with women of the other indigenous peoples. This kind of marriage in itself determined the need for trade exchange and, as a consequence of this process, the establishment of foreign political alliances.

Food products, mats, skins, feathers of rare birds, various kinds of tools from seashells, valuables obtained from sunken Spanish ships, as well as captives - all this travelled from Florida to Cuba and Yucatan for trade purposes. "They (the Calusa - K.A.) are skilled sailors," wrote Andres Gonzalez de Barcha. – Their boats filled with fish, fruits and skins regularly sail from the Keys (Florida Keys archipelago - K.A.) towards Havana. They usually get there within 24 hours. Trade with the Arawak's (the Indian people of South America, individual groups of which inhabited Cuba - K.A.) makes them even richer and more powerful..."

Fig. 45A. *The found canoes of the Florida Indians. Photo by K. E. Ashrafyan*

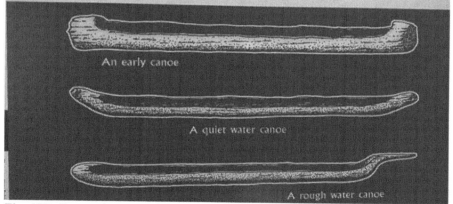

Building a Canoe

The Calusa made canoes out of a single log. To shape the boat, they burned the middle and chopped out the charred wood with robust shell tools. They used other shell tools to finish the surfaces.

An early canoe

A quiet water canoe

A rough water canoe

Fig. 45B. *Types of canoes of Calusa. Photo made in the Bishop Museum of Science and Nature (formerly the South Florida Museum), Bradenton, Florida, USA. Photo by K.E. Ashrafyan.*

45C. The canoe, which is probably several thousand years old, was discovered after a drought in Florida at the end of the 20th century. Photo from the film "Dugout Canoes-The opening of 101 canoes on Lake Newnan, Florida, USA", Youtube, URL: https://www.youtube.com/watch?v=9UNrck45OtE

Fig. 45A, B, C. The canoes of the Florida Indians (presumably the canoe of the Calusa Indians). Wooden canoes are well-preserved in the Florida aquatic environment. Canoes hollowed out of a single trunk have been found in many places, but the largest and most impressive find was made at Lake Newnan near Gainesville, where more than 100 pieces of the canoes which were discovered during the drought. Most of the canoes are made of pine, but there is also cypress.
Photo by K. E. Ashrafyan

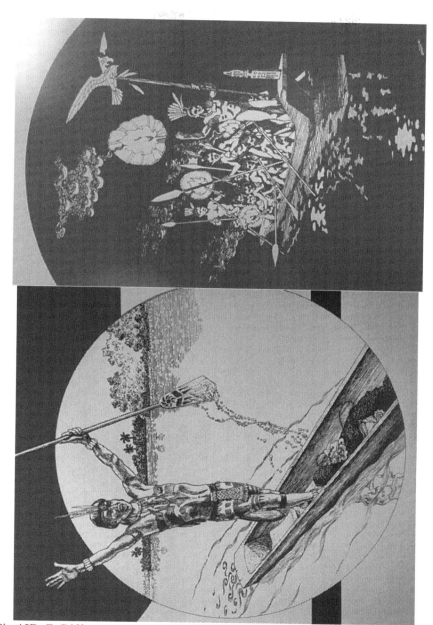

Fig 45D, E. Different canoes of Calusa tribe. Stand in the Museum of Gainesville.
Photo by the author

Fig. 46A. Canoes in the form of a catamaran, which are held together by a platform in the middle, on which goods and cargo were transported

Fig. 46B. Canoes with the platform in the middle on which important people were transported

Fig. 46A, B. Various types of boats of the Kalusa people. The Florida Museum of Natural History and the South Florida Museum (Bishop's Modern Museum). Photo by K. E. Ashrafyan

WHAT THE CALUSA INDIANS LOOKED LIKE?

The Calusa people, as chroniclers noted, were quite tall: men - 180 cm and above, and women: 160 cm but the Spaniard's height was average160–165 cm, So, the Indians seemed a whole head taller! The height, athletic build and facial features of the representatives of this people contrasted sharply with the Taino Indians and Arawak Indians (the average height of people of the Arawak and Taino men approximately 160-165 cm and women around 150-155 cm which inhabited Hispaniola, Cuba, Caribbean islands.

The Calusa Indians wore long, flowing hair, but men sometimes wore their hair in a ponytail or tied it in a knot at the back of the head (Fig. 47).

Men usually wore tanned buckskin loincloths the width of a human palm, covering their loins. A woman's loincloth, or, as Spanish sources indicate, a "skirt," was made from moss ("Spanish moss" or "Louisiana moss") or fibers from palm leaves. "The Indians of the large islands are well-built," Fontaneda wrote. "Their women are figure well-built, piquant, and not ugly. They walk naked, only a small bandage the width of a palm made of deerskin barely covers the lower back of the men. A woman covers her loins with aprons made of a certain type of grass (moss - K.A.), growing on trees, similar to wool..." [32].

Another Spanish traveller Andres Gonzalez de Barcha in the 1690s. described the Calusa Indians this way: "They all, without exception, walk naked. On the thighs of both men and women there are rags of plant origin. Their hair is long. Women wear their hair loose and never braid it. Men tie their hair in a knot. Their instincts are vile and vicious, their eyes sparkle with unhealthy lust, which they do not hide".

Necklaces made from shark teeth, small shells and bird bones were common among Calusa jewellery. "They made small holes at the ends of the ...shell, in the area of the cone, - wrote de Barcha. - After which they threaded them on a thread and got beads that the Indians wore around their necks and for which they could exchange everything they needed with other tribes". The flat parts (disks) of mollusc shells were also used by the Indians as decoration. This type of boa was worn by caciques and was known as an attribute that emphasized their status in society.

Kings, warlords, and priests of Calusa wore headdresses decorated with intricate designs of beads and feathers. "Their chief king, Carlos," wrote de Avilés, "stood out from other nobles with his outward pretentiousness. A lean athlete, on whose body, in addition to prominent muscles, one could see a fancy colouring, emphasizing the nobility of his origin. The king's head was decorated with a crown of multi-coloured feathers. On the hoop in the centre of the frontal part of the crown there was a carved tablet (Fig. 48). The hair was collected at the top of the head and secured with clips from bone. The upper and lower parts of the face are fragmentary painted with black paint. There are also designs on the shoulders and forearms, framed by bracelets made of beads and colourful shells. The king's neck is hung with pearl necklaces of different diameters. Carlos's back was covered with a cape of dyed bunting feathers. A bearskin stocking was pulled over one of the legs. The lower back was covered by a red belt woven from the fibers of some plant."

In the chronicles of Florida Governor Menendez de Aviles there is also a description of Carlos's wife: "The king's wife is hung from head to toe with beads made of pearls, precious stones, and gold. The forehead... is decorated with a circlet of gold plate in the centre, and the legs with beaded bracelets."

During the holidays, the noble women of Calusa painted their bodies red, which emphasized their nobility and membership in the royal clan and wore everything associated with their jewellery. Commoners decorated their bodies and faces with ornaments. Shell beads and shark tooth pendants were shaped on her chest, and a pair of bird feathers were woven into her hair.

It should be noted that, according to the chronicler Governor Menendez, the women of the royal family had the right to vote, in particular the elder sister of the chief-king, who after her baptism was called Doña Antonia, openly expressed her disapproval of the actions of both her brother-chief and her new husband - Governor Menendez [64].

As for the tattoo culture of the Calusa Indians, from the surviving records of the Spaniards it can be understood that only members of the nobility, priests and warriors had designs on their bodies that reflected their status. On holidays, all Indians of the tribe painted their bodies black, white and red, which were obtained from local plants, such as Florida arrowroot (arrowroot). It is unlikely that the Indians had body paintings applied to them every day, that is, since in their daily lives they were engaged in fishing and were constantly exposed to water, which would wash away the applied paint, although they had a lot of time for self-development and enjoyment.

"The life of the Calusa was very leisurely and measured," Fontaneda noted, "they enjoyed celebrations and holidays, many of which had religious significance. They prepared lavish dinners and did not forget to decorate themselves with jewellery".

Fig. 47A. Illustrations depicting the Indians of South Florida, made by M. Clark and T. Morris. Photo by the author from different museums of Florida.

Fig. 47B. Images of warriors created by the author using AI (artificial intelligence) Midjourney and edited by Ashrafyan K.

Fig. 47C. The women of South Florida. Photo from the Bishop Museum of Science and Nature (formerly the South Florida Museum), Bradenton, Florida; photo from a painting from the Florida Museum of Natural History in Gainesville; installation in Fort de Soto Park, Bradenton, Florida, USA. Photo: Ashrafyan K.E.

Fig. 47D. Bas-relief with images of Florida Indians in the Municipal Parking Centre in St. Petersburg, Florida, USA.
Fig. 41 A, B, C, D. *Images of Florida Indians*

Fig. 48. The King of the Calusa tribe, Carlos, is receiving guests. Reconstruction, Florida Museum of Natural History. Photo by K. E. Ashrafyan

RICHES OF LAND AND WATER RESOURCES

Despite the fact that the Calusa Indians led a sedentary lifestyle, scientists classify their economic and cultural type as fisher-hunter-gatherers.

Calusa planted small gardens on the territory of cities located in the vicinity of the lake Okeechobee. There they grew cabbage, tobacco, papaya, peppers, and possibly cassava. Scientists have found no evidence that the Calusa grew crops such as corn. V. Marquardt, explaining the lack of legumes and grains in the Calusa diet, refers to documents from the Narvaez expedition of 1528, which provide facts regarding the fact that the Calusa did not accept agricultural tools from the Spaniards, telling the Spaniards that they were not needed.

The coastal waters of western Florida were rich in marine resources that provided the basis for the Calusa towns located in the region. The Calusa were completely dependent on the sea. Their diet consisted of 80% seafood, which they caught in coastal waters. As a Spanish chronicler wrote in 1566, when meeting with the Spaniards, the Calusa were served "many kinds of very good fish, fried and stewed, and raw, stewed and fried oysters" [64]. 20% of the Calusa diet consisted of food products - the fruits of wild plants (dates, prickly pear cactus, purslane, mallow, etc.), berries (sea grapes, wild plums, palmetto, dogwood, etc.), acorns and various root vegetables. vegetables (wild potatoes) [56].

The world of Calusa was a world of sea fishing and hunting. All members of the community took part in seafood production. Women and children collected clams, oysters, and fish-like snails. Men used spears and nets to catch mullet, tuna, whales, lobsters, turtles, sharks, hammerheads, manatees, shrimp, and other marine life (Fig. 49).

The black mullet (Mugil Cephalus, mullet), given its feeding and schooling behaviour, high meat production and good fat content, was a fish used by the Calusa for mass fishing and the production of surplus feed [80]. Mullet lend themselves well to culture in fish ponds due to their ability to obtain nutrition at the base of the food chain from diatoms and other algae found in the substrate and sometimes in the water column of Gulf of Mexico estuaries [46].

For their excellent fishing skills, the Spaniards called the Calusa "Pescadores grandes" - "great fishermen" (Fig. 50).

According to Fontaneda and de Avilés, the Calusa also bred crocodiles, alligators, and turtles, which "were something like pets for them." The Indians not only ate reptile meat, but also traded it. Combs were made from turtle shells, and bags for household needs, as well as quivers and sheaths for arrows, were made from crocodile skin.

Fig. 49. The "Great fishermen" ("Los grandes pescadores") of Calusa. Florida Museum of Natural History. Illustration by M. Clark

Fig. 50. Delivery of fish by canoe along the canal, Florida Museum of Natural History. The illustration by M. Clark

To catch marine life, the Calusa made nets from palm fibers of various sizes. To corral fish, dams were built from shellfish shells. At high tide, the fish found themselves in a pen, the exit from which was blocked by nets. For direct catching of fish, spears and lances were used, as well as wooden fishing rods, the hooks of which were the teeth of predatory fish; turtles were caught using sucker fish.

The population of cities located at the mouths of rivers and swampy backwaters of the interior regions of Florida, in addition to river and sea fish, which were delivered from coastal areas, also consumed the meat of wild animals: deer, bears, water rats, snakes, etc. [63]. Many animals had ritual significance - they were totems or emblems of clans, some were intended to decorate and highlight representatives of the highest Indian nobility [56], as was later the case with the Seminole Indians.

Usually, Calusa people harvested animal meat and products for future use: the meat was smoked over a campfire and then stored in earthen refrigerators; fruits were dried, berries were crushed, cooking something like jam. Tobacco was one of the oldest crops grown by indigenous. Tobacco was highly valued among the Indians and was considered a sacred plant (in fact, a drug), which, when used in large doses, caused hallucinations in the priests, allowing them to come into contact with spirits and receive "revelations" or advice from them.

In all scientific works, the authors argue that the existence of such a powerful regional socio-political complex, created at one time by the Calusa Indians without using elements of agriculture (agriculture and animal husbandry — K.A.), is mainly due to the exceptionally rich coastal habitat. However, research recently indicates that the environment in which the Calusa society found itself changed over time, leading to changes in the sociocultural practices of these Indians. The Calusa were forced to adapt to changing environmental parameters over long periods of time. In this regard, they were forced to transform their belief system, based on ancient traditions, knowledge, and experience of the tribal elders.

The changing environment and experiences of previous generations allowed them to improve their engineering skills, which undoubtedly improved their standard of living and contributed to the expansion and strengthening of international ties. All this as a whole helped the Calusa to remain a prosperous people and dominate the region even during times of various crises.

TOOLS, HUNTING AND WEAPONS OF CALUSA

Calusa's tools are of undoubted interest. Among the artifacts found by archaeologists are many sharp scrapers, pottery shards, flint arrowheads, flint knives, skilfully crafted mollusc shells, shark teeth, and various beads. These "riches" were found in the so-called "garbage heaps", high artificial mounds - living evidence of the Calusa culture that has survived to this day.

The Calusa Indians made tools for labour and hunting from wood, flint, shells, bones, teeth of sharks and other predatory fish (Fig. 51A and 51B). Their habitat contained no hard rock other than soft limestone, so the "*green stone*" for Calusa wedges or axes was obtained through barter and trade from Indians living in the northern part of what is now the state of Georgia.

Among the objects that the Calusa fought with, it is worth noting the atlatl - a simple and effective weapon that the Calusa skilfully used for military purposes and in hunting [2, p. 278–280]. It was no less formidable than the arquebuses of the Spaniards, better than a bow and arrow and more effective than an ordinary spear, since it reached speeds of up to 130 km/h (Fig. 51C, D).

The Spaniards, who saw gold and silver jewellery among the Calusa, only assumed their local origin. Gold and silver deposits have never been discovered in Florida (small amounts of gold were discovered in the late 19th century in northeast Florida). Modern scholars believe that Calusa gold, silver, copper, and brass items were acquired through intertribal trade.

The Calusa were not only fierce warriors, but also creators. Calusa pottery, which included freshwater spicule sponges, quartz crystals, shell rock and limestone, was very durable. This composition protected the product from cracking during firing and increased its safety. After firing, the products were polished with small pebbles or other hard objects until they acquired shades of red pigment.

In addition to ceramics, they made exquisite wooden dishes, ritual masks, figurines of animals, boa constrictors, and were well-known for their skill in bone carving. Products made by the Calusa from materials obtained from the sea were in exceptional demand in the north of the peninsula, as well as on the mainland of Southeastern of North America. Archaeologists have found perfectly cut shells made by Calusa craftsmen as far away as Oklahoma, and small shell beads and flint knives of extraordinary sharpness have been found in Indian villages in Ohio and Indiana.

Fig 45A. Reconstruction of swords using shark teeth and turtle rattles. Exhibition at De Soto Park, Florida, USA, 2015

Fig. 45B. Bow, atlatl, arrows etc., Reconstruction of enthusiast De Bari. Exhibition at De Soto Park, Florida, USA, 2015

Fig. 51C. The replica artifact from Key Marco, Collier County, Florida, USA. It was the weapon or possibly a cutting tool made from shark teeth. Florida Museum of Natural History.

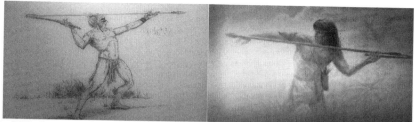

Fig.51D. Images of Indians throwing spears (short spears) from atlatl. The figures show two different ways of archery.

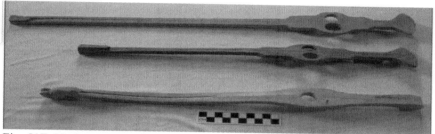

Fig. 51E. Various types of atlatls from Florida. Replicas: at the top – the longest and most successful shape with two finger holes; in the middle – a shortened one, also with two finger holes; at the bottom – with a stand in the form of a hare's tail and with one hole for holding

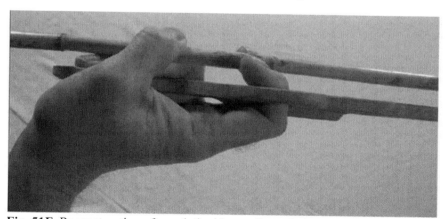

Fig. 51F. Reconstruction of an atlatl with two finger holes, showing how the dart inserted into the atlatl was held and how it lay in the hand

Рис. 51A, B, C, D, E, F. Various types of weapons of the Calusa Indians – replicas and reconstructions. Photo by K. E. Ashrafyan

CAPITAL AND OTHER SETTLEMENTS

Let us recall that modern science learned about the Calusa people quite recently - in the twentieth century. There is still a lot of work and research to be done. At the moment, archaeologists have been able to discover several settlements of this disappeared people, three of which are the largest: Mound Key, Pineland and Marco Key (Fig. 52).

Human presence on the island. Pineland arose in the 1st century, i.e., in the favourable climate of the Roman warm period [63, p. 806–827].

In 500–850 a cool period sets in, sea levels drop, which leads to a shortage of resources in the shallow estuarine systems of the area [60]. Then the natives begin to build auxiliary canals to feed the reservoirs around the mound in Pineland.

At the same time, the types of florida dwellings began to change from small, probably single-family dwellings dating from the late Caloosahatchee I period to larger multifamily structures.[81] Around 900, at its peak, Pineland Island was home to about 1,000 people in 16 large houses [63].

But the medieval warm period brought hurricanes and storms that, among other things, destroyed a third of the barrier islands. Pineland [76]. These events gave impetus to the development of a geographically more conveniently located island. Mound Key.

By the time the Spanish first landed on the coast of Florida, Mound Key was the main unifying and defensive centre of the Calusa people. This is a fairly large island with an area of 51 hectares, located in the centre of Estero Bay (Fig. 53).

As mentioned earlier, Mound Key was settled in the early 6th century. By the 10th century, a significant change in the landscape of the island had occurred: the construction of the Grand Canal began on two large mounds, 6 m and 10 m high, located in the centre of the island (the canal ran directly between the mounds). Soon a network of canals covered the entire island.

In the southern part of the island, two large reservoirs (fish storage facilities) were built, which, as scientists suggest, contained live surplus fish from river mouths [84].

"The King's House" (Fig. 54), the largest house of Calusa, built on a 10-meter mound, was rebuilt at least 3 times: the early stage of construction - 995-1140; average – from 1165 to 1400; late - from 1395 to 1570, including perestroika - in 1500-1513. [33; 108].

The building had an oval shape with a diameter of about 24 m along the long axis and 20 m along the short axis [57; 79], capable, according to the Spaniards, of accommodating more than 2000 people [90, p. 247]. The house stood on 150 pillars located at 0.25–0.5 m from each other and made of pine (Pinus taeda - "southern hard" or "yellow" pine), brought to the island especially for this purpose [79; 43]. The area of the house was about 380 m^2. It appears that this is not much, but it is quite enough, considering that the structure had several tiers.

Pedro Menendez de Aviles, who visited Mound Key in 1566, described the house of King Carlos: "...the house is large enough to accommodate 2000 people without crowding. This house also served as a meeting place for nobles and priests who helped the king make important decisions. When I entered the house, I saw before me Carlos sitting on a high throne, surrounded by 500 noble men, and also his sister-wife on the throne next to him, surrounded by 500 noble wives." The testimony of two friars who found themselves in the house of the cacique Calusa in 1697 speaks of two large windows in the house, as well as a roof made of palm leaves that "leaked when it rained."

There was another type of house in the city - houses on stilts, which arose primarily due to constant flooding from storms and tropical rains, typical of the west coast of Florida. Secondly, such a structure of houses protected residents from attacks by amphibians and other predators and parasites [100].

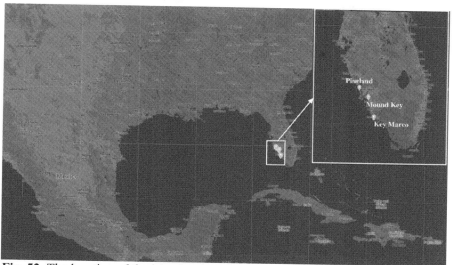

Fig. 52. The location of the islands where intensive excavations were carried out in South Florida, USA: Pineland, Mound Key and Key Marco

Fig. 53A. Mound Key Island. Engraving, 1896

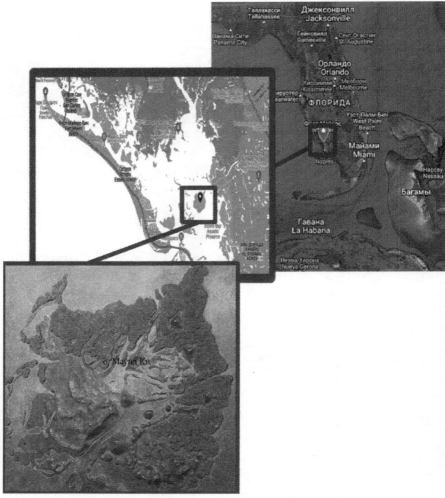

Fig. 53 B. The model of the island of Mound Key

Fig. 53A, B. The image of the island of Mound Key. Florida Museum of Natural History. Photo by K. E. Ashrafyan

Fig. 54A. The house exterior of the King of Calusa. Illustration by M. Clark

Fig. 54B. The King of Calusa - Carlos is surrounded by the nobility. Photo by the author from Florida Museum of Natural History.

Fig. 54C. The device of the roof of the house of King of Calusa.

Fig. 54A, B, C. The house of the King of Calusa, or the "King House" in Mound Key. Florida Museum of Natural History

The Calusa Indians drove long wooden piles into shell foundations to give them stability. A wooden platform was installed on stilts, on which stood a hut, the roof of which was covered with dwarf palm branches or thatch. The shady space under the house was used for storage.

The method of creating foundations for houses from available natural materials was later adopted from the Calusa Indians by the Spanish who built their fortifications in Florida. For the foundation, the Aboriginal people used shells and marl (a type of clay), which, when mixed and dried, produced a material comparable to modern concrete. From the same mixture of shells and marl, the Indians made blind areas, sidewalks, ramps and other elements of urban architecture. Moreover, the Calusa traded this building material, delivering it by boat along riverbeds and dug canals to the cities of their fellow tribesmen who lived in the interior of the peninsula.

The canals, according to scientists, were an important means of communication and a unique engineering structure of the Calusa civilization. These waterways were located very close to the houses of the Indians, which created certain amenities, and were used by the Indians as urban "streets" along which passengers and various cargoes were transported by boats (Fig. 55). The usual channel width was 35 feet (10.67 m).

These waterways connected not only the quarters of the town, but also the canals connected villages throughout the territory of Calusa, which allowed not only to quickly supply settlements with goods, but also to quickly assemble an army. Archaeologists claim that in the east, between the lakes, there was also a network of canals built by Calusa between Lake Okeechobee and Charlotte Harbor Bay.

The construction of houses on high embankments allowed the Calusa to control vast areas around, quickly detect any danger, send sound, light or other signals to other settlements, quickly mobilize and, thanks to the flotilla of canoes at their disposal, evacuate from the danger zone. In addition, due to the specifics of the settlement structure and living in large houses of several hundred people, it was not difficult for the Calusa Indians to quickly assemble a large military force of several hundred people. And with the presence of neighbouring settlements, it was possible in a short time to field an army of several thousand people to defend or attack enemies.

All these features of the structure of society gave Calusa advantages over other aborigines who inhabited Florida. The high artificial hills were an ideal viewing platform. And the houses in which many residents lived were a prototype of barracks with a good surveillance system and rapid mobilization of soldiers and the population. The canal system and large fleet of canoes contributed to Calusa's dominance in Central and Southern Florida.

The Mound Key complex was the centre of the Calusa Indians for many centuries, where at certain times of the year many Calusa people gathered, who at one time settled throughout the Florida Peninsula from Tampa Bay in the north to the south of the Florida Peninsula, and to Lake Okeechobee, located on east of the Gulf of Mexico.

Today, mounds and "middens" of shells and other tribal remains, many covered in subtropical vegetation, are the only visible evidence of the Calusa people who once dominated South Florida and their way of life.

Fig 55. Engineering structures of the Calusa Indians are smooth channels connecting different parts of the islands and settlements on the mainland. The Randall Research Center in Pineland, Lee County, Florida. Photo by K.E. Ashrafyan.

CONCLUSIONS

THE GENERAL CONCLUSIONS

The formation of the Calusa, a politically complex chiefdom (or "primitive state based on tribute") created by the hegemon tribe, became possible thanks to the organization of the vertical "Power in society" or "Pyramids of power" (fig. 38), founded for organization within the state. The creation of a separate layer of permanent warriors was done to maintain order, wage constant wars, and suppress any centrifugal tendencies emanating from other South Florida settlement leaders who tried to pursue an independent policy.

We now know that by early 1350 AD, corresponding to the period of the Caloosahatchee IV culture, the settlement of Mound Key became the political and religious centre of the Calusa people, from which the hegemonic tribe extended its influence into the interior of the country and coastal areas of western, southern, and Southeastern Florida.

Already in the first years of the 16th century, the Calusa first learned about Europeans from the natives from the West Indies who fled from the Spaniards to the south of the Florida peninsula and directed their efforts to organize a union of tribes capable of resisting the Spaniards.

The resulting alliance of the peoples of South Florida was able to organize successful resistance from the

1500s to the 1700s to European attempts to organize the penetration and subjugation of South Florida, as the Calusa united the peoples and tribes of South Florida around themselves. This became possible because the Calusa refused trade ties, religious penetration, military-political cooperation, and any other types of interaction with the Spaniards and other Europeans, and also prevented any attempts by Europeans to land in south Florida.

The success of the Calusa as a hegemony tribe was due to the very location of the tribe's settlement at the mouths of Florida rivers and the creation of a vertical power structure within the established society of fishermen, hunters, and gatherers (FHG). The unique society that arose, unlike other agricultural and pastoral societies, did not depend on the weather conditions necessary for the ripening of crops or the germination of grass, and did not even depend on the seasonal conditions of the arrival and departure of fish into the sea. The estuaries formed in Florida, unique in nature, turned Calusa into a settled society that provided food for all residents because it consisted of 80% of naturally and artificially replenished marine resources.

The decline and disappearing of the Calusa people contradict the established formula that it was only "white men and European diseases that completely exterminated the entire population of Florida". It is clear from the history of this people that this occurred as a result of the mass extermination of the Calusa people by the invading tribes of the Yamasee, Creek and other Indian tribes and peoples, who mercilessly destroyed the Calusa Indians themselves, captured them and sold them into slavery to the British or simply killed them.

The territory of central and southern Florida was deserted only in the XVIII century after constant attacks and destruction of the local population by other Indian tribes invading from the north. The vast expanses of desert Florida were quickly settled by the Creek Indian tribes and the Seminole tribes descended from them.

Florida has always been a tasty morsel for all European countries - Spain, France, England, as it was of strategic importance for controlling shipping from the New World to Europe and controlling the Caribbean. Its development was an important moment for the development of the whole of North America. And the fact that the Calusa successfully defended their independence for 250 years, without having any firearms and living in complete isolation, was truly an extraordinary phenomenon.

RESEARCH PERSPECTIVES BASED ON THE REFERENCE POINTS OF THE DEVELOPMENT OF THE CALUSA SOCIETY

Currently, scientists have not found any documents indicating the presence of writing of the Calusa people. But the history of the tribe tells us that there had to be a letter and a counting system! It is enough to take a sober look at the development of Calusa: throughout the millennial existence of civilization, the Calusa society has been constantly developing, and the transfer of knowledge was necessary to each other for many reasons. For instance, consider the sophisticated mass construction of houses and structures - the existence of a large system of properly constructed canals connecting populated areas over a large area was discovered and proven. Fisheries and fish reproduction were also developed: pen systems for growing and breeding fish, places for storing and processing fish for a large number of community members and for sale and exchange, production of a large number of nets, hooks, sinkers, floats, etc.

Knowledge and writing were needed in the pyramidal-hierarchical system of society, a society with the divine role of cacique kings, where there was a hereditary aristocracy, a system of beliefs with constant rituals and strict worship of their gods, the need to convey laws and faith to commoners (artisans, fishermen, hunters, gatherers). The same system of organizing society and performing work in this society presupposes the development of laws and the need to give orders over long distances, store and carry out precise instructions for performing complex work and carry out calculations for the redistribution of received material wealth in society.

But there was also an almost professional army that collected tribute and waged external wars. This army needed discipline, it needed uniforms and weapons, and it needed reports on the conduct of wars - on the losses and gains that had occurred, somehow it was necessary to organize the provision of food and weapons and other items of income and expenses. It is also necessary to take into account the network of subordination of other tribes with elements of tribute, which cannot function without a system of counting and managing the process. It is also important to consider the features of architectural structures - the creation of large buildings which could accommodate from 50 to 2000 people. These were not primitive shacks, but multi-tiered strong and reliable buildings - houses for the community and high society, religious buildings of the priests. This required a school of its craftsmen and the transfer of experience from generation to generation, the generation and improvement of tools for the construction of structures. This involves the transfer of knowledge and calculations, since the structures were built on shell mounds in the area of the island, where there are annual and frequent hurricanes, floods, torrential tropical downpours and other Florida-specific conditions, and where primitive buildings would simply collapse at the first blow of the elements.

The most interesting evidence of the transfer of experience and the growth of professional skills in Calusa is the production of exquisite and complex hunting paraphernalia, wooden mechanical masks for hunting animals and birds, etc., the production of various types of canoes specially adapted for hunting and traveling through swamps, rivers, and sea, carried out both for oneself and for exchange or sale to other tribes, which requires a good production base and the transfer of knowledge. Also, the version about the existence of a system of counting and the transfer of knowledge through some kinds of writing leads to good navigational practice of long-distance voyages of the Spanish sailors of the Calusa and established cooperation and trade with neighbouring Yucatan and along the Mississippi, described in the chronicles of the 16th century.

The transfer of names is also evidenced by the presence of a list of names of rivers, lakes, bays, and other settlements remaining from the Calusa language, some of which are still preserved on geographical maps.

All of the above areas of Calusa life require the storage and transmission of knowledge, professional skills in calculation and accounting of material values, as well as the dissemination of laws and decrees among the population from generation to generation. And, as we now understand, knowledge can be transmitted not only in the form to which we are accustomed - in the form of inscriptions or cuneiform writing on walls, papyrus, bark or other media, but they can also have original systems, for example, knot writing (weaving), pictography, ideography, writing puzzles, stone carving, tattoos and so on.

The Calusa language has little survival in speech, gestures, facial expressions, and sounds, although some research has been conducted in the 20th century. Perhaps there were some other types of information transmission over long distances, and not only the already known signal sounds of shells, drums, and fire... all this will probably be carefully studied and summarized in the future.

It is clear that there was oral learning, visual, practical, mentoring, etc., but still some knowledge acquired in written form was probably also present.

Considering that after the complete extermination of the peoples of Florida in the 17th and 18th centuries, the existence of the disappeared Calusa civilization became known only in the 20th century, it is safe to say that unexpected discoveries in this direction await us in the future. Unfortunately, the barbaric, but necessary for the development of the Florida region, destruction of the coastal strip as a result of the construction of roads and highways has reduced the chances of finding and studying the lost civilization.

But... Thanks to science enthusiasts and humanity's desire for knowledge, everything is in our hands... and there will definitely be a sequel and new discoveries!!!

APPENDIX 1. THE PEOPLE WHICH DESCRIBED OR MENTION THE CALUSA TRIBE

- Hernando de Escalante Fontaneda (1536-1575) – he spent 17 years (1549 - 1566) in captivity among the Calusa Indians and was an interpreter for the Governor of Florida, Menendez de Aviles [102].

- A Portuguese man named Gentleman Elvas, a member of the Hernando de Soto expedition, who wrote memoirs about the expedition [40].

- Gonzalo Solís de Merás - chronicler of the first Governor of Florida and Cuba (1565–1574) - Pedro Menéndez de Avilés (1519-1574) [64].

- Andrés González de Barcia (1673-1743), real name was Andrés Gonzalez de Barcia Carballido y Zuniga [98].

- Bartolomé de las Casas (1484-1566). He was Spanish clergyman known for his work as an historian and social reforme in New World [9].

- Jonathan Dickinson (1663-1722). He had shipwrecked on the southeast coast and held captive by tribe Jeaga or "Jobe" ("Hoe-bay") for several days [29].

- Alvar Nunez Cabeza De Vaca (1488-1559) one of four survivors of the 1527 Narvaez expedition and during eight years (1528-1536) of traveling across territory modern USA and Mexico[46].

- Jacques de Morgues Le Moyne (1533-1588). He was a French artist and a member of Jean Ribot's French expedition 1562 and French expedition by Rene Goulaine de Laudonnière in 1564 to the Florida.

---

[46] Alvarez Nunez Cabeza de Vaca. Shipwreck, Moscow Miysl. 1975, 128 p.URL: https://libking.ru/books/nonf-/nonf-biography/1061644-alvar-nunes-kabesa-de-vaka-korablekrusheniya.html#book.

APPENDIX 2. THE FORMULA OF INTERESTS

The formula of interests made by the author based on the analysis and generalizations of various Indian uprisings in the XVI century [121].

$$(A \times (D + E)) + B + C = \sum.$$

The formula shows the perniciousness of the lack of mixing of Spaniards and natives, that is, the absence of an important "gender factor" in the "formula of expectation" of local leaders from an alliance with the Spaniards and the consequences of negating all the components that correspond to the formula we have deduced: $(A \times (D + E)) + B + C = \sum$.

A is the establishment of the hegemony of the local leader through a military alliance with the Spaniards.

B – the prestige of the tribal leader among his fellow tribesmen.

C – the possibility of exchanging new goods (iron tools for cultivating the land, iron axes, swords, knives, etc.).

D – the "gender factor" – the possibility of acquiring nepotism with Europeans (stronger in the technical development of weapons), by creating marriage alliances with women from their tribe; E – the adoption of a new (Christian) religion by tribal leaders, members of their families.

$\sum$ – the strength of the alliance and interest between the local chiefs and the Spaniards.

Four stages in the development of relations between Indians and Spaniards:

1) Establishing a relationship based on mutual interest and benefit.
2) The development of relations and mutual obligations of the parties.
3) The **"gender factor"** as a turning point in the conflict of relations.
4) The uprising of indigenous

The addition to the Appendix 2.

An important "gender factor" that the Spaniards did not want to take into account was taken into account by the French in 1704, when the founder of the fort in Alabama, Bienville (**Jean-Baptiste Le Moyne de Bienville**) realized that the cohabitation of local girls and women with French soldiers would lead to conflict between the male local population of French settlers. And this could lead to an uprising of the aborigines. Bienville went so far as to arrange the arrival of twenty-four young French women recruited from monasteries and poor families. These girls are known in local stories as **casket girls** or **casquette girl** in early stories and in English translation.

APPENDIX 3. "THE INDIAN HERITAGE TRAIL"

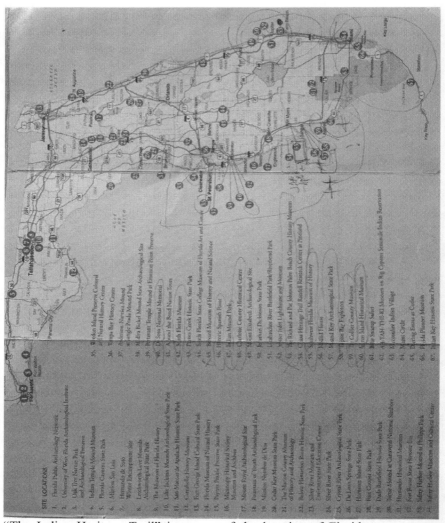

"The Indian Heritage Trail" is a map of the location of Florida museums and historic sites, a component of the Florida Indian Heritage Trail, a non-profit Florida membership network whose mission is to provide public education and visitation to Florida's historic heritage sites.

SOURCES AND LITERATURE

1.   Akimov, Yu. G. The discovery of Florida and the beginning of Spanish economic expansion in the southeastern part of the North American continent in 1510 = Otkry`tie Floridy` i nachalo ispanskoj e`kspansii v yugo-vostochnoj chasti Severoamerikanskogo kontinenta v 1510-e gody`. SPb : ILA RAN. 2013. pp. 58–69.

2.   Aleksandrenkov, E. G. Aborigines of the Greater Antilles in colonial society: The end of the XV – the middle of the XVI century = Aborigeny` Bol`shix Antil`skix ostrovov v kolonial`nom obshhestve: Konecz XV – seredina XVI veka. Bel`cy: Parmarium Academic Publishing, 2017. 508 p.

3.   Castilyo, B. D. The true story of the Conquest of New Spain = Pravdivaya istoriya zavoevaniya Novoj Ispanii. Moskva: Forum, 2000. 678 p.

4.   Kofman, A.F. Knights of the New World = Ry`czari Novogo Sveta. M.: Pan Press, 2006. 200 p.

5.   Kofman, A. F. The Spanish conquistador. From text to personality type reconstruction = Ispanskij konkistador. Ot teksta k rekonstrukcii tipa lichnosti. Moskva: IMLI RAN, 2012. 304 p.

6.   Kofman, A.F. America of Unfulfilled Miracles = Amerika nesby`vshixsya chudes. Moskva, 2001. 347 p.

7.   Kofman, A.F. Konkistadory`: tri xroniki

zavoevaniya Ameriki. per. s isp. Andreya Kofmana i Evgenii Ly`senko. Moskva, 2009. 606 p.

8. Kofman, A.F. Under the patronage of Santiago. The Spanish conquests of America and the fate of the famous conquistadors = Pod pokrovitel`stvom Sant`yago. Ispanskie zavoevaniya Ameriki i sud`by` znamenity`x konkistadorov. Sankt-Peterburg: Kriga, 2017. 1030 p.

9. Las Kasas B. de. History of the Indies = Istoriya Indij : [sokr.] per. s ispan. / otv. red. D. P. Priczker, G. V. Stepanov [i dr.] Leningrad, 1968. 113 p.

10. Smolenskij, N. I. Problemy` metodologii istorii: ucheb. posobie dlya stud. vy`ssh. ucheb. zavedenij = Problemy` metodologii istorii: ucheb. posobie dlya stud. vy`ssh. ucheb. zavedenij / N. I. Smolenskij. 2-e izd., stereotipnoe. Moskva: Izdatel`skij centr «Akademiya», 2008. 272 p.

11. Yarovoj, E. V The secret of small nations. From Basques to Bushmen = Tajny` maly`x narodov. Ot baskov do bushmenov. Moskva : Veche, 2019. 285 p.

12. Yarovoj, E. V. The disappeared peoples of the world = Ischeznuvshie narody` mira. Moskva : Veche, 2019. 320 p.

13. Yarovoj, E. V. In the footsteps of ancient treasures Po sledam drevnix kladov. Moskva. Veche, cop. 2010. 348 p.

14. Alegre, Francisco Javie Historia de la Provincia de la Compañía de Jesus de Nueva España. Tomo I. Roma: Institutum Historicum S.J. 1956, 640 p.

15. Ames, K.M. Myth of the Hunter-Gatherer. Archaeology Magazine, September/ October, 1999. pp. 45–49.

16. Arnold, J.E., Sunell, S., Nigra, B.T., Bishop, K.J., Jones, T., Bongers, J., Entrenched Disbelief: Complex Hunter-Gatherers and the Case for Inclusive Cultural Evolutionary Thinking. Journal of Archaeological Method and Theory 23, 2016. 448–499.

17. Beck, R. A. The durable house: material, metaphor, and structure. In: Beck, R.A. (Ed.), The Durable House: House Society Models in Archaeology. Center for Archaeological Investigations, Carbondale: Southern Illinois University, 2007. pp. 3–24.

18. Bennett, C. E. Settlement of Florida. Geinesville: University of Florida, 1968. 253 p.

19. Blanton, R.E., Fargher, L.F., How Humans Cooperate: Confronting the Challenges of Collective Action. University Press of Colorado, Boulder. 2016. 436 p.

20. Brown, J.A., Kelly, J.E., Surplus labor, ceremonial feasting, and social inequality at Cahokia. In: Morehart, C., de Lucia, K. (Eds.), Surplus: The politics of production and the strategies of everyday life. University

Press of Colorado, Boulder, 2015. P. 221–244.

21. Cahokia and the Hinterlands: Middle Mississippian Cultures of the Midwest / Emerson, E. T, Lewis, B. R. First Edition. *Urbana-Champaign*: University of Illinois Press, 1999. 376 p.

22. Clark, M.R., Marquardt, W.H. The Archaeology of Pineland: A Coastal Southwest Florida Site Complex, A.D. 50–1710. Gainesville, 2012. 944 p.

23. Coffman, F. L.V. Atlas of Treasure Maps: [Over 3000 Location of Sunken or Buried Treasures In The Western Hemisphere & Britain] Nashville, 1957. 126 p.

24. Colección de documentos inéditos relativos al descubrimiento, conquista y organizacion de las antiguas posesiones españolas de América y Oceania, T. XXII / Bajo la dirección de los Sres. D. Joaquín F. Pacheco y D. Francisco de Cárdenas y D. Luis Torres de Mendoza; Archivo General de Indias. Madrid: Imprenta de Manuel G. Hernandez, 1874. 577 p.

25. Covington, J.W., 1959. Trade relations between Southwestern Florida and Cuba, 1600–1840. Florida Historical Quart. 38, P. 114–128.

26. Cushing, F. H. Exploration of ancient key dwellers' remains on the gulf coast of Florida, New York: Published by AMS Press for Peabody Museum of Archaeology and Ethnology, Harvard University, Cambridge, Mass. 1973, 161 p.

27.   Cushing, F. H. Preliminary Report on the Exploration of Ancient Key-dweller Remains on the Gulf Coast of Florida // Proceedings of The American Philosophical Society. Philadelphia: The American Philosophical Society, 1896. P. 329-448.

28.   Cushing, F.H. Exploration of ancient key dweller remains on the Gulf Coast of Florida. Proc. Am. Philosoph. Soc. 35, 1897. 329–448 p.

29.   Dickinson, Jonathan Dickinson's Journal or, God's protecting providence. Being the narrative of a journey from Port Royal in Jamaica to Philadelphia between August 23, 1696 and April 1, 1697. Gainesville: Port Salerno, Fla. : Florida Classics Library, 1985. 172 c.

30.   Edgar, B. W. South Carolina: A History. First Edition. Columbia: University of South Carolina Press, 1999. 776 c.

31.   Elbert, L., Little, Jr., of the U.S. Department of Agriculture, Forest Service - USGS Geosciences and Environmental Change Science Center: Digital Representations of Tree Species Range Maps from: Elbert L. Little, Jr., Atlas of United States trees, Vol. 4, minor Eastern hardwoods: U.S. Department of Agriculture Miscellaneous Publication 1342, 1977. 17 p., 230 maps.

32.   Ellis, J.T. Documents of American Catholic History. Volume 1. 1493-1865. Wilmington: Michael Glazier, 1987. 268 c.

33.   Episodic complexity and the emergence of a coastal kingdom: Climate, cooperation, and coercion in Southwest Florida. Journal of Anthropological Archaeology. 2022. № 65 (101364). P.1-28.

34.   Ethridge, R. From Chicaza to Chickasaw: The European Invasion and the Transformation of the Mississippian World, 1540–1715. New edition. Chapel Hill: The University of North Carolina Press, 2010. 360 p.

35.   Fletcher, J.W. The history of Cuba. New York : B.F. Buck & company, inc., 1920. 438 p.

36.   Fuson, R.H. Juan Ponce de León and the Spanish discovery of Puerto Rico and Florida. Blacksburg, Va: McDonald & Woodward Pub, Co. 2000. XVI, 268 p.

37.   Gallay, A. The Indian Slave Trade: The Rise of the English Empire in the American South 1670–1717.Kindle edition. New Haven: Yale University Press, 2002. 464 p.

38.   Gannon, M. The cross in the sand: the early Catholic Church in Florida. 1513–1870. Gainesville, 1965. XV, 210 p.

39.   Garcilaso de la Vega La Florida del Ynca: historia del adelantado Hernando de Soto, Gouernador y capitan general del Reyno de la Florida, y de otros heroicos caualleros españoles è indios. Madrid: Impresso por Pedro Crasbeeck, 1605, 702 p.

40.   Hakluyt, R. The discovery and conquest of

Terra Florida by Don Ferdinando de Soto and six hundred Spaniards his followers, written by a gentleman of Elvas, employed in all the action, and translated out of Portuguese by Richard Hakluyt. Reprinted from the edition of 1611, edited with notes and an introduction, and a translation of a narrative of the expedition by Luis Hernandez de Biedma / Richard Hakluyt, Luis Hernandez de Biedma, William B Rye. London: Printed for the Hakluyt Society, 1851. 281p.

41.   Hann, J.H. A History of the Timucua Indians and Missions. Gainesville, 1996. 400 p.

42.   Hann, J.H. Indians of Central and South Florida 1513–1763. Gainesville, 2003. 249 p.

43.   Hann, J.H. Missions to the Calusa /(Columbus quincentenary series) (Ripley P. Bullen series). Gainesville: University of Florida Press : Florida Museum of Natural History, 1991. XIX, 460 p.

44.   Hann, J.H. The Native American world beyond Apalachee: West Florida and the Chattahoochee Valley. Gainesville, 2002. P. 250.

45.   Herrera y Tordesillas A. Historia general de los hechos de los castellanos en las Islas y Tierra Firme del mar Océano que llaman Indias Occidentales. Madrid: 1601. P. 303.

46.   Hiatt, R.H. Food-chains and the food cycle in Hawaiian Fish Ponds. Part 1. The food and feeding habits of mullet (Mugil cephalus), milkfish (Chanos chanos), and

the ten-pounder (Elops machnata). Transactions of the American Fisheries Society 74 (1), 1947. P. 250–261.

47. Hudson, C. M. Black Drink: A Native American Tea. Athens : University of Georgia Press, 2018. 184 p.

48. Indians of the greater Southeast: historical archaeology and ethnohistory / Edited by McEwan, G. B. 1 edition. Gainesville: University Press of Florida, 2000. 522 p.

49. Jennings, J., Earle, T.K., Urbanization, state formation, and cooperation: a reappraisal. Curr. Anthropol. 2016. 57, P. 474–493.

50. Laudonnière, R. G. A foothold in Florida the eye-witness account of four voyages made by the French to that region and their attempt at colonisation, 1562-1568, based on a new translation of Laudonnière's L'Histoire notable de la Floride. Antique Atlas Publications, West Sussex, England. 1992. P. 234 p.

51. Luer, G. M. Royal W. R. Florida Anthropological Society. 2013. №51 (1). P. 47–48.

52. Luer, G.M., Wheeler, R.J., How the Pine Island Canal worked: topography, hydraulics, and engineering. Florida Anthropol. №50, 1997. P. 115–131.

53. Macmahon, D. A. The Calusa and Their Legacy: South Florida People and Their Environments (Native Peoples, Cultures, and Places of the Southeastern

United States) / D. A. Macmahon, W. H. Marquardt. Geainesville : University Press of Florida, 2003. 240 p.

54.   Marcus, J. The archaeological evidence for social evolution. Annual Review of Anthropology. Redwood City: Stanford University Press. Tomo 37, 2008, P. 251–266.☐

55.   Marley Wars of the Americas: A Chronology of Armed Conflict in the New World, 1492 to the Present. Santa Barbara : ABC-CLIO, 1998. 722 p.

56.   Marquardt, W. H. Politics and production among the Calusa of south Florida / Marquardt, W. // Hunters and Gatherers, Vol. 1: History, Evolution, and Social Change (Explorations in anthropology). New York : St. Martin's Pres, 1988. P. 160-186.

57.   Marquardt, W. H., Walker, K. J., Thompson, V. D., Savarese, M., Thompson, A. D. R., & Newsom, L. A. Episodic complexity and the emergence of a coastal kingdom: Climate, cooperation, and coercion in Southwest Florida. Journal of Anthropological Archaeology, 2022. V.65, Article №101364.

58.   Marquardt, W.H. Politics and Production among the Calusa of South Florida. In: Ingold, T., Riches, D., Woodburn, J. (Eds.), Hunters and Gatherers, Vol. 1: History, Evolution, and Social Change. Berg Publishers, London, 1988. P. 161–188.

59.   Marquardt, W.H. The Calusa social formation

in protohistoric South Florida. In: Patterson, T.C., Gailey, C.W. (Eds.), Power Relations and State Formation. Archeology Section, American Anthropological Association, Washington, DC, 1987. P. 98–116.

60. Marquardt, W.H. Tracking the Calusa: a retrospective. Southeastern Archaeol. 33, 2014. P. 1–24.

61. Marquardt, W.H., Trade and Calusa complexity: Achieving resilience in a changing environment. In: Ling, J., Chacon, R., Kristiansen, K. (Eds.), Trade before civilization: Long distance exchange and the development of social complexity. Cambridge: Cambridge University Press,. In press. 2022. P. 173-206.

62. Marquardt, W.H., Walker, K.J., Southwest Florida during the Mississippi period. In: Ashley, K.H., White, N.M. (Eds.), Late Prehistoric Florida: Archaeology at the Edge of the Mississippian World. University Press of Florida, Gainesville, 2012. P. 29–61.

63. Marquardt, W.H., Walker, K.J. The Pineland site complex: an environmental and cultural history. In: Marquardt, W.H., Walker, K.J. (Eds.), The Archaeology of Pineland: A Coastal Southwest Florida Site Complex, A.D. 50-1710. Institute of Archaeology and Paleoenvironmental Studies, Monograph 4. Gainesville: University of Florida, 2013, P. 793–920.

64. Meras, G. S. Pedro Menendez de Aviles and the conquest of Florida: a new manuscript / Gonzalo Solís

de Merás; edited, translated, and annotated by David Arbesú-Fernández. Gainesville: University Press of Florida, 2017. XII, 431 p.

65. Milanich, J. T. Florida Indians and the Invasion from Europe. Gainesville : University Press of Florida, 1995. XIX, 290 p.

66. Mitchem, J.M., & Moore, C.B. The West and Central Florida Expeditions of Clarence Bloomfield Moore. Tuscaloosa: The University of Alabama Press, 1999. 934 p.

67. Moore, C.B. Certain antiquities of the Florida west-coast. J. Acad. Nat. Sci.Philadelphia 11, 1900. P. 350–394.

68. Morris T. Florida's Lost Tribes / with commentary by Jerald T. Milanich. Gainesville, 2004. 70 p.

69. Oviedo y Valdez G. F. Historia general y natural de las Indias, islas y tierra-firme del mar océano. Vol. 2. Madrid, 1853. 651 p.

70. Palov, M.Z., 1999. Useppa's Cuban fishing community. In: Marquardt, W.H. (Ed.), The archaeology of Useppa Island. Institute of Archaeology and Paleoenvironmental Studies, Monograph 3, University of Florida, Gainesville, P. 149–169.

71. Peck, D. T. Ponce de León and the discovery of Florida: the man, the myth, and the truth. Saint Paul,

Minn.: Pogo Press, 1993. 87 p.

72. Peckham, H. H. Colonial Wars, 1689-1762 (The Chicago History of American Civilization). 3rd Printing edition . Chicago: University of Chicago Press, 1965. 266 p.

73. Pineland. The Archaeology of Pineland: A Coastal Southwest Florida Site Complex, ca. A.D. 50–1710 / ed. by W. H. Marquardt and K. J. Walker. Gainesville, 2013. 944 p.

74. Pineland during the Spanish Period. A Mechanical Waterbird Mask from Pineland and the Calusa Masking Tradition // The Archaeology of Pineland: A Coastal Southwest Florida Site Complex, ca. A.D. 50 – 1710 / ed. by W. H. Marquardt and K. J. Walker; Institute of Archaeology and Paleoenvironmental Studies, University of Florida Gainesville. – Gainesville, 2013. P. 1–22.

75. Societies in Eclipse: Archaeology of the Eastern Woodlands Indians, A.D. 1400-1700 / D. S. Brose, R. C. Mainfort Jr. , C. W. Cowan, Dr. Marvin T. Smith, S. Williams, D. G. Anderson, J. Bradley , P. B. Drooker , G. R. Milner , D. H. Thomas , D. R. Snow, R. P. Davis Jr , H. T. Ward, C. W. Johnson. J. L. Hantman, W. R Fitzgerald, R. C. Mainfort , R. F. Sasso , W. H. Marquardt , W. H. Marquardt и др.; под ред. Brose, D. S. . - Tuscaloosa: University Alabama Press, 2005. 304 p.

76.   Stapor Jr., F.W., Mathews, T.D., Lindfors-Kearns, F.E., 1991. Barrier-island progradation and Holocene sea-level history in Southwest Florida. J. Coastal Res. 7 (3), 1991. P. 815–838.

77.   Swanton, J. R. The Indian tribes of North America. Bureau of American Ethnology, Bulletin 145, Government Printing office. Washington, 1952. 726 p.

78.   The La Salle Expedition to Texas: The Journal of Henri Joutel, 1684 1687 // William Foster (Editor), Johanna S. Warren (Translator). Denton: Texas State Historical Assn, 1998. 360 p.

79.   Thompson, V.D., Marquardt, W.H., Cherkinsky, A., Roberts Thompson, A.D., Walker, K. J., Newsom, L.A., Savarese, M., From shell midden to midden-mound: The geoarchaeology of Mound Key, an anthropogenic island in Southwest Florida, USA. PLoS ONE 11 (4). 2016. P. 1-22

80.   Thompson, V.D., Marquardt, W.H., Savarese, M., Walker, K.J., Newsom, L.A., Lulewicz, I., Lawres, N.R., Roberts Thompson, A.D., Bacon, A.R., Walser, C.A., Ancient Engineering of Fish Capture and Storage in Southwest Florida. Proc. Natl. Acad. Sci. V. 117 (№15) 2020. P. 8374-8381.

81.   Thompson, V.D., Marquardt, W.H., Walker, K.J., 2014. A remote sensing perspective on shoreline modification, canal construction and household trajectories

at Pineland along Florida's southwestern Gulf Coast. Archaeol. Prospect. 21, 2014, P. 59–73.

82. Thompson, V.D., Thompson, A.R., Marquardt, W.H., Walker, K.J., Newsom, L.A., Reitz, E.J., 2020b. Discovering San Anton de Carlos: The sixteenth-century Spanish buildings and fortifications of Mound Key, capital of the Calusa. Historical Archaeol. 54 (2), 2020. P. 334-353.

83. Thompson, Victor D., Marquardt, William H., Walker, Karen J., Roberts Thompson, Amanda D., Newsom, Lee A., Collective action, state building, and the rise of the Calusa kingdom. Journal of Anthropolpgical and Archaeol. №51 2018. P. 28–44.

84. Trade before Civilization: Long Distance Exchange and the Rise of Social Complexity. Ling J., Chacon R. J., Kristiansen K. (Eds.) Cambridge: Cambridge University Press, 2022. 446 p.

85. Turner, S. Juan Ponce de León and the Discovery of Florida Reconsidered. *The Florida Historical Quarterly*. 2012. T. 92, № 1. P. 1-31.

86. Wheeler, R.J. Treasure of the Calusa: The Johnson/Willcox collection from Mound Key, Florida. Monographs in Florida Archaeology, Tallahassee: Rose Printing, 2000. 187 p.

87. Widmer, R.J. The Evolution of the Calusa: A Nonagricultural Chiefdom on the Southwest Florida Coast.

Tuscaloosa: University of Alabama Press, 1988. 352 p.

88.   Widmer, R. J. Introduction. Exploration of Ancient Key-dweller Remains on the Gulf Coast of Florida. By Cushing, F. H. Gainesville: University Press of Florida, 2000. 161 p.

89.   Wood J.M. A History of the Catholic Church in the American South 1513-1900. Gainesville: University Press of Florida, 2011. 512 p.

90.   Worth, J. E. Discovering Florida: First-Contact Narratives from Spanish Expeditions along the Lower Gulf Coast. University Press of Florida. Gainesville, 2016. P. 43–86.

91.   Worth J.E. The Lower Creeks. Origins and Early History. // Indians of the Greater Southeast: Historical Archaeology and Ethnohistory (Co-published with The Society for Historical Archaeology). Chapter 10. - Gainesville: University Press of Florida, 2001. P. 265-298.

92.   Worth, J. E. A History of Southeastern Indians in Cuba, 1513-1823 / J. E. Worth // unpublished paper presented at the Southeastern Archaeological Conference. 2004. P. 1-17.

93.   Worth, J. E. Fontaneda Revisited: Five Descriptions of Sixteenth Century Florida [Электронный ресурс] / J. E. Worth // The Florida Historical Quarterly. 1995. T. 73, № 3. P. 339-352.

94.   Worth, J. E. Pineland during the Spanish Period, in: Marquardt, W.H., Walker, K.J. (Eds.), The Archaeology of Pineland: A Coastal Southwest Florida Site Complex, A.D.50-1710. Institute of Archaeology and Paleoenvironmental Studies, Monograph 4. Gainesville: University of Florida, 2013, P. 767–792.

95.   Zubillaga F., Rodríguez, M. A. Monumenta Mexicana, Roma: Apud "Monumenta Historica Soc. Iesu", 1956. 610 p.

96.   Zubillaga, F. La Florida: la misión jesuítica (1566-1572) y la colonización espanola. Roma : Institutum Historicum S.I., 1941. 473 p.

ARCHIVES

97.   AGI. [Documento   PATRONATO,19,R.32: Relación de todos los caciques de la Florida. [Fecha de creación] 1565, Sevilla.

ONLINE SOURCES AND LINKS TO ONLINE LITERATURE

98.   Cardenas y Cano, Gabriel de (**González de Barcia Carballido y Zúñiga, Andrés**) Ensayo para la historia de la Florida contiene los descubrimientos y principales sucesos acaecidos en este gran Reino á los

españoles, franceses, suecos, dinamarqueses, ingleses, y otras naciones entre sí, y con los indios; cuyas costumbres, genios, idolatría, gobierno, batallas y astucias se refieren; y los viages de algunos capitanes y pilotos por el mar del Norte á buscar paso á Oriente, ó unión de aquella tierra con Asia, desde el año 1512 que descubrió la Florida Juan Ponce de León hasta el de 1722 (1723) / y. C. Cárdenas. Текст : электронный // BIBLIOTECA DIGITAL HISPÁNICA : [сайт]. URL: http://bdh-rd.bne.es/viewer.vm?id=0000124731&page=1 (date of access: 08.12.2023).

99.   D'Arrigo, R., Klinger, P., Newfield, T., Rydval, M., Wilson, R., 2020. Complexity in crisis: The volcanic cold pulse of the 1690s and the consequences of Scotland's failure to cope. J. Volcanol. Geoth. Res. 389, 106746. URL: https://doi.org/10.1016/j.jvolgeores.2019.106746 (date of access: 05.12.2023).

100.   Dye, D. H. (1977). Review: The Material Culture of Key Marco Florida. American Anthropologist. URL: https://www.academia.edu/84489528/Review_The_Material_Culture_of_Key_Marco_Florida (date of access: 07.12.2023).

101.   Fitzmaurice-Kelly J. Trozos escogidos de la Florida del Inca. ARREGLADOS Y SELECCIONADOS. Oxford: Oxford, University Press, 1921. URL:

https://archive.org/details/trozosescogidosd00vega/page/n3/mode/2up (date of access: 09.12.2023).

102. Fontaneda H. De Memoria de las cosas y costa y indios de la Florida, que ninguno de cuantos la han costeado, no lo han sabido declarar. URL: http://www.cervantesvirtual.com/obra/memoria-de-las-cosas-y-costa-y-indios-de-la-florida-que-ninguno-de-cuantos-la-han-costeado-no-lo-han-sabido-declarar--0 https://biblioteca.org.ar/libros/131873.pdf (date of access: 08.12.2023).

103. González de Barcia Carballido y Zúñiga, Andrés. Origen de los Indios de el Nueuo Mundo, e Indias Occidentales. / de, Barcia, Carballido,y González. Текст : электронный // Internet Archive : [сайт]. URL: https://archive.org/details/origendelosindio00garc/page/n5/mode/2up (date of access: 08.12.2023).

104. Lopez C. Appropriation or Acculturation? Spanish Influence on Calusa. URL: http://dpanther.fiu.edu/dpService/dpPurlService/purl/FI180 50900/00073 (date of access: 08.12.2023)

105. Peck D.T. Misconceptions and Myths Related to the Fountain of Youth and Juan Ponce de Leon's 1513 Exploration Voyage / Peck, Douglas. URL: https://web.archive.org/web/20080409062720/http://www.newworldexplorersinc.org/FountainofYouth.pdf (date of access: 25.11.2021).

106. Rogel, J. First Hand Accounts of Virginia, 1575-1705. Carta de Juan Rogel / Rogel Juan. Текст : электронный // Virtual Jamestown : [сайт]. URL: https://web.archive.org/web/20030304230405/http://etext.lib.virginia.edu/etcbin/jamestown-browse?id=J1038 (date of access: 29.11.2023).

107. Rogel, Juan. "Letter from Juan Rogel to Francis Borgia (August 28, 1572)" // Encyclopedia Virginia URL: https://encyclopediavirginia.org/entries/letter-from-juan-rogel-to-francis-borgia-august-28-1572/ (date of access: Thu, Nov 24., 2023).

108. Thompson, V., Marquardt, W.H., 2015. Report on Archaeological Investigations at Mound Key (8LL2) (2013 and 2014 Field Seasons), Lee County. Committee for Research and Exploration, National Geographic Society, Washington, DC Florida URL: https://www.floridamuseum.ufl.edu/rrc/blog/archaeological-investigations-at-mound-key-2013-and-2014/ (date of access: 08.12.2023)

THE AUTHOR'S PUBLICATIONS ON THE RESEARCH TOPIC

109. Ashrafyan K. E. The chronology of the discovery and development of Florida in the 16th century

Part 2: The first stage of the discovery and development of Florida from 1513 to 1516 in: Bulletin of Moscow Region State University. Series: History and Political Sciences, 2023, no. 2, pp. 65–78

110. Ashrafyan, K. Problem points of various research methods and prospects for their solution in the study of Spanish Florida of the XVI-XVIII centuries // "Revista Transilvania" January. 2022. T. 4. № 2022. pp. 86–96.

111. Ashrafyan, K. The extinct Calusa tribe as the hegemon of south Florida in the xvi–xvii centuries: reasons for its military leadership among other aborigines of Florida // Samara Journal of Science. 2020. V. 9. № 1(30). pp. 159–164.

112. Ashrafyan, K. Two views at the "Fountain of Youth" as the main reason for organizing an expedition to discover new lands in the first quarter of the XVI century. // Science, innovation, society in modern conditions. Monograph. Penza: MCNS «Nauka i Prosveshhenie», 2022. pp. 122–135. (Chapter 11)

113. Ashrafyan, K. The lands of the Florida Indians in the middle of the xvi century: map of the leaders of Florida according to the memoirs of Hernando de Fontaneda // The best Scientific research work. 2021. Penza, MCNS «Nauka i Prosveshcenie», 2021. pp. 107—111.

114.   Ashrafyan, K. (2022). Spanish colonization of Florida in the first quarter of the 16th century: methods, features, causes of failure (English version) // [Zenodo]. URL: https://doi.org/10.5281/zenodo.7452063.

115.   Ashrafyan K. Images of Indians from Spanish Florida in the XVI century. Truth and lies, speculation and facts.: [Report at the meeting of the Russian–American Research Forum NEXUS II, session 3] / Konstantin Ashrafyan, PhD student at Moscow State Regional University. - 04/23/2021. – Oral speech, image: electronic // Anthrotube (Antropologiya = Anthropology): [chanal of YouTube]. URL: https://www.youtube.com/watch?v=7Hcw5CzJVq

116.   Ashrafyan, K. The history of translations of the "Memoirs" and other texts by Fernando de Escalante Fontaneda: the history of translations, comments, and drawings to the text // Gumanitarny`j nauchny`j vestnik. 2021. T. 8. № 2021. pp. 1–7.

117.   Ashrafyan, K. Chapter 11. The disappeared tribes of Florida as an urgent issue of modern science and education: the need to get out of oblivion of knowledge about the history of American peoples of the "pre-seminol era" // Topical issues of modern science and education monograph. Penza, Russia: MCNS «Nauka i prosveshcenie», 2021. pp. 125–140.

118.   Ashrafyan, K. Chapter 17. Translation of the

text "memories" ("memoir") by Hernando de Escalante de Fontaneda into Russian: a story about the tribes of Florida in the mid-XVI century // Innovations in science, society, education. Monograph. Penza, Russia: MCNS "Nauka i Prosveshchenie", 2021. S. 203–219.

119.   Ashrafyan, K. Information about the settlement and making of the aborigen tribes on the Florida peninsula in the XVI century: a history of return from non-existence // The best scientific work of 2021: a collection of articles of the XXXII International Competition of scientific papers, which will be held on August 15, 2021 in Penza. MCNS «Nauka i Prosveshcenie», 2021. pp. 44–55

120.   Ashrafyan, K. A new view of the native uprisings in Spanish Florida and the West-Indies in the XVI century ("The gender factor" and "expectation formula" in the XVI century native uprisings in Spanish Florida and the West-Indies) // Samara journal of science. 2020. V. 9. № 2 (2020). pp. 158—167.

121.   Ashrafyan, K. History of Florida by… Myths and Heroes. 1511-1513 / K. Ashrafyan. — 1st ed. — Charleston : Create Space Publisher, 2016. — Vol. 2. — 332 p. — History of Florida by…. — ISBN 978-1541342743

122.   Ashrafyan, K. History of Florida by… Fountain of Youth 1513-1514 / K. Ashrafyan. — 1st ed. — Charleston : Create Space Publisher, 2016. — Vol. 3.

— 325 c. — History of Florida by.... — ISBN 978-1542459525.

123. Ashrafyan, K. Spanish Florida: peoples, expeditions, and the effects of struggles and epidemics in the XVI and early XVII centuries. // Aktual'ni problemi vitchiznyanoï ta vsesvitn'oï istorii 2019. № 22. P. 34-44.

Review of Dr. K.E. Ashrafyan's monograph

Professor E.V. Yarovoy

The relevance of the work

The relevance of the presented monograph lies in the fact that such topics are rarely found in Russian historiography.

Scientific novelty and main results

This work is devoted to the culture of the Caloosahatchee and the Calusa tribe that existed from the 5th century AD to the XVIII century and disappeared in the "abyss of time". At the same time, it considers and quite convincingly substantiates the possibility of the existence of a separate region in the south of the Florida Peninsula. This region was inhabited by Indian tribes with different histories of origin, among which the Calusa tribe occupied an important place. This tribe, which became dominant in southern Florida, unlike other Indian tribes of the North American continent. They managed to unite and preserve their culture, way of life, religion, and traditional way of life. In the conditions of expansion into the North American continent of Spain and other European states from the XVI century to the XVIII century. Which is an interesting fact and an example of resilience in today's historical realities. This work objectively shows how the discovery of the land called Florida at the beginning of the XVI century led to numerous attempts to develop this land by the Spaniards, the French and then the British. These same attempts to establish a permanent settlement in the Spanish Flora led to the consolidation of the tribes of southwestern and southern Florida under the leadership of the Calusa tribe. And this, in turn, led to important consequences for navigation from the New World to Europe for all ships of European countries, forced to avoid calls to the southwest and south of the Florida Peninsula. It is extremely important that when revealing the topic, the author personally visited the sites of the events that took place and examined the artifacts presented in various museums, their replicas, and copies, as well as studied a large layer of existing, new and little-known materials and documents stored in various libraries, museums, and archives in Europe and the USA, to one degree or another, they highlight the origin and main trends of the Spanish colonization of Florida and the resistance to this from the Indian tribes living there. The introduction of certain concepts into scientific circulation in Russian historical science, such as the "silver age of piracy" in the Atlantic, the "Florida hegemony tribe" and the "Formula of interest in contacts between the leaders of local tribes and Europeans" and the concept of "fishing hunter-gatherer societies" already existing in English-speaking countries is an absolute merit the work done by the author. It should also be noted that the maps and images of the Indians of Florida generated by the author.

The positive aspects of the monograph

A positive aspect of the work is the disclosure of the reasons that allowed the people of Calusa to defend their right to exist. In the conditions of a hostile and highly organized and technically more advanced environment of enemies - the Spaniards, the French, and the British. K.E. Ashrafyan managed to reasonably prove that the images of Indians are Florid used so far in publications on historical sites. The sites were fictional and created by the enemy of the Spaniards – the German Protestant, engraver, and publisher Theodore de Brie, who had never been to America and had not seen the real aborigines of Florida. Another positive aspect of this work is a new look at the causes of the disappearance of many tribes of North America. Not as a result of confrontation with colonists (Spaniards, French or British) or imported diseases of white people, but as a result of raids by Indians of the Creek, Yamasee, etc. tribes armed with English firearms who destroyed, or Florida Indians. They were taken captive for further sale into slavery on plantations to English colonists or to the West Indies. It is also indicated that any contact between Europeans and the Indians of the Calusa tribe was impossible due to a unique sedentary society, atypical for other regions of the world, the Calusa fishing-hunter-gatherer society. It despised agricultural labor and had in its daily diet more than 80% of the food obtained from the waters of the Gulf of Mexico. It should be emphasized that these conclusions are based on a detailed analysis of various artifacts and documents of that era, obtained, and presented in museums in Florida and archives in Spain and the United States.

Disadvantages of the work

The only comment that can be made to this work is to the title of the work. The name is too cumbersome, it can be formulated more succinctly: "Calusa or the vanished civilization of South Florida." In the presented work, K.E. Ashrafyan showed himself to be an active and professional scientist. He was able not only to clearly formulate the goals and objectives of his research, but also to successfully implement them, using all the possibilities available to him. His ability to work professionally with sources and scientific literature should also be noted.

Conclusion and summary of the work

K.E. Ashrafyan has done a lot of work on the collection, classification, and analysis of extensive factual material. It is important to note that there are very few serious and comprehensive studies on the history of the peoples of the "Spanish Florida" in the Soviet and Russian scientific literature to date. This monograph significantly closes this "white spot", and not only in Soviet and Russian historiography. I believe that the work meets all the requirements for scientific papers and should be recommended for publication.

The reviewer: Professor of the Department of Universal History, Federal State Educational Institution of Higher Education "State University of Education" **Doctor of Historical Sciences, Professor E.V. Yarovoy**

PROFESSOR S.I. RESNYANSKY

Relevance of the work

This monograph is dedicated to the people of South Florida who disappeared in the XVIII century, known as the "Calusa". Recently, this topic has aroused increased interest not only in the scientific community, but also among the public in various countries. This interest is caused by the desire to find out the causes and consequences of the disappearance of indigenous peoples who lived not only in southern Florida, but also in other regions of the North American continent. In this regard, it is extremely difficult to overestimate the relevance of this monograph.

Scientific novelty and main results

Extensive study of the topic allowed the author to involve numerous literature and sources on this topic in the analysis. K.E. Ashrafyan not only published and, thus, introduced many previously unknown sources into scientific circulation, but also gave them a detailed historical analysis. It should also be noted the successful description of the history and culture of the Calusa people, which for the first time in the historiography of the CIS countries are presented on such a scale. In this regard, the presented monograph compares favorably with most previously published works, both in Russia and abroad.

The positive sides

Among the many fundamental conclusions of the author, it should be especially noted that he managed not only to clarify, but also to explain why the Indian society of Calusa developed differently from other North American societies. He was able to organize an alliance of Florida tribes, which successfully resisted the Spanish conquistadors. In addition, the author managed to show the causal links between the wars of Spain, England, Holland, and France in the Old and New World and the raids of various tribes of Southeastern North America. This led to the disappearance of the indigenous tribes of South Florida, including the Calusa.

Disadvantages of the work. During the work on the monograph, the author was pointed out that in some cases his style of presentation was characterized by excessive verbosity and not obvious formulation of individual conclusions. However, all the comments he made were considered when finalizing this monograph.

Conclusion and summary of the work

As a result of a deep and methodically logical analysis of extensive factual material, the author managed to come to very unexpected, but convincingly reasoned conclusions. Among the most important of these, it should be noted that by the beginning of the 14th century, the Calusa people had already formed a political and religious center. Their influence spread to the interior and coastal areas of western, southern, and Southeastern Florida. At the same time, the formation of the Kalusa took place - a politically complex chiefdom created by a hegemony tribe, which allowed for more than 200 years to successfully resist the penetration of Europeans and Christian ideas into South Florida. And the decline of the Calusa people came only with a wave of brutal raids by the Creek and Yamasee Indian tribes. They destroyed many people of Florida, selling them into slavery on plantations to English colonists or to the West Indies.

The presented monograph "Calusa, or the disappeared civilization of the hegemony tribe of South Florida" has an absolute novelty associated with the publication of numerous documents on this topic, many of which were discovered and prepared for extensive publication by the author personally; it has undeniable practical significance for the further development of this topic and related issues. Problems that are especially relevant in modern conditions. This work can be safely recommended for use in the educational process at the historical, geographical and international faculties of various universities, in particular, in the preparation of special courses and seminars on world history.

The reviewer: Professor of the Department of History,
Federal State Educational Institution of Higher Professional Education "State Pedagogical University"
Doctor of Historical Sciences, Professor S.I. Resnyansky

ACKNOWLEDGMENTS

I would like to express my great gratitude for the creation of this monograph to the editor of the scientific journal Svetlana Yu. Polyakova, without whose enthusiasm the presentation would be too bland and, in many ways, paler than what the reader can see now. Correctly posed numerous questions to me as the author of the monograph, forced me to disclose important information in more detail to the reader and give explanations of incomprehensible points. Thanks to her professionalism and enthusiasm, the text, links, and illustrations of this monograph were formed.

I would also like to express my gratitude to Sergey Konstantinovich Konev, a professional designer, for many years of cooperation and the creation of the cover.

I would like to express my gratitude to Dr. John Worth from the University of West Florida, Dr. Jerald Milanich and Dr. William H. Marquardt from the University of Florida, Dr. Chet Van Duzer from University of Rochester, as well as artists Theodore Morris, Douglas Peck (son of Douglas T. Peck) for their cooperation and recommendations, for their works to study History of Florida. I would like to express my gratitude to Prof. E.V. Yarovoy and Prof. V.E. Baghdasaryan for giving me the opportunity to explore at the university a rare topic about Florida, which had not previously been raised in the post-Soviet space and in the CIS countries on the history of the discovery of Florida and the disappeared peoples of the "pre-Seminole period". I express my gratitude for the consultations, their work, correspondence support, and a vector in the direction of research to Dr. E.G. Alexandrenkov, Dr. A. Yu. Petrov, Dr. Yu.G. Akimov, Dr. S. I. Resnyanskiy, Dr. A. F. Kofman, Dr. N.I. Smolensky, Dr. A.V. Fedin, Ph.D. A.V. Kalyuta, Ph.D. A.S. Klemeshov, Ph.D. N.A. Yasnitsky and PhD D.V. Mikheev and PhD Y.V. Solovyov and PhD N.V. Deynega and other scientists with whom fate brought me together during the writing of this monograph. I would like to express special gratitude to all the staff of the libraries of the University of Florida, the University of South Florida, the Russian State Library, the University of St. Petersburg. Leo is in Florida, and the employees of the General Archives of Spain for their enthusiasm and interaction with me.

I would also like to say a word of gratitude to those enthusiasts, thanks to whom information about the tribes of South Florida appeared in literature outside the academic scientific field. And first of all, I would like to express my gratitude to the Belarusian writer I. Kostyan for his numerous stories on the portal: https://proza.ru/avtor/cowboy1967.

It is impossible to ignore and express admiration for the excellent and tremendous work of the creators and editors of the important Internet resource "The World of Indians" [https://www.indiansworld.org], where there is an association of historians and enthusiasts interested in the Native American culture of the American continent, who selflessly give their time and inspire enthusiasm in many people, infecting them with the "Indian spirit" and research in the depths of history.

ALL ARTICLES AND BOOKS OF ASHRAFYAN KONSTANTIN EDUARDOVICH (ENGLISH VERSION)

ARTICLES

1 Ashrafyan K. The considering the discovery of Florida in 1513. In: Bulletin of the Moscow Regional State University. Series: History and Political Sciences, 2020, no. 2, pp. 166–174.
DOI: 10.18384/2310-676X-2020-2-166-174
https://www.istpolitmgou.ru/jour/article/view/117/117
https://doi.org/10.18384/2310-676X-2020-2-166-174
https://doi.org/10.5281/zenodo.5303563
https://archive.org/details/httpsdrive.google.comdriveu3fol
ders1qhaepb-xscnqpftmxekfwnfwloglpr77

2 Ashrafyan, K. The extinct Calusa tribe as the hegemon of south Florida in the XVI–XVII centuries: reasons for its military leadership among other aborigines of Florida //

Samara Journal of Science. 2020. V. 9. № 1(30). pp. 159–164.
URL: https://doi.org/10.5281/zenodo.5304209
https://archive.org/details/httpsdrive.google.comdriveu3fol
ders1qhaepb-xscnqpftmxekfwnfwloglpr77_202008

3 Ashrafyan, K. A new view of the native uprisings in Spanish Florida and the West-Indies in the XVI century ("The gender factor" and "expectation formula" in the XVI century native uprisings in Spanish Florida and the West-Indies) // Samara journal of science. 2020. V. 9. № 2. pp. 158—167.
URL:https://snv63.ru/2309-4370/article/view/41950/pdf
DOI: 10.17816/snv202203
URL DOI: https://doi.org/10.17816/snv202203
ZENODO DOI: https://doi.org/10.5281/zenodo.5307883
URL: https://snv63.ru/2309-4370/article/view/41950/pdf
ZENODO URL: https://doi.org/10.5281/zenodo.8424730
URL:
https://archive.org/details/httpsdrive.google.comdriveu3fol
ders1qhaepb-xscnqpftmxekfwnfwloglpr77_20200804

4 Ashrafyan, K. Spanish Florida: peoples, expeditions, and the effects of struggles and epidemics in the XVI and early XVII centuries. // Actual problems of national and world history. Collection of scientific papers. 2020. V. 22. № 2020. pp. 34–44.
URL:
https://archive.org/details/httpsdrive.google.comdriveu3fol
ders1qhaepb-
xscnqpftmxekfwnfwloglpr77_20200804_1347
Zenodo URL: https://doi.org/10.5281/zenodo.5236382

5 Ashrafyan, K. Spanish Florida: peoples, expeditions, and the effects of struggles and epidemics in the XVI and early XVII centuries. // Actual problems of national and world history. Collection of scientific papers. 2020. V. 22. pp. 34–44.
URL:
https://archive.org/details/httpsdrive.google.comdriveu3fol ders1qhaepb-
xscnqpftmxekfwnfwloglpr77_20200804_1347
https://doi.org/10.5281/zenodo.5236382

6 Ashrafyan, Konstantin, Beznosov, Mikhail. "Black legend" as a tool of the geopolitical struggle in XVI century and its interpretation today: the denigration of the enemy-country and modern the strategy of demonizing // Bulletin of the Moscow Region State University. Series: History and Political Sciences. 2021. V. 2. № 2021. pp. 125–138.
URL: https://doi.org/10.5281/zenodo.8424521

7 Ashrafyan, K. Slavery and freedom of the natives of the New World at the beginning of the XVI century as a result of the policy of confrontation between the Spanish crown and the "House of Columbus". 2020. European Scientific Conference (MK-954), Penza, Russia. pp. 95—101
Zenodo URL: https://doi.org/10.5281/zenodo.5260914

8 Ashrafyan K.E. «The Silver Age of Piracy»: French pirates in the Atlantic in the first third of the XVI century // Samara Journal of Science. 2020. Vol. 9. N. 4. pp. 232-239.
DOI: 10.17816/snv202094204. EDN OZIZCO.

URL:
https://elibrary.ru/download/elibrary_44617484_22684762.
pdf
Zenodo URL: https://doi.org/10.5281/zenodo.8423289
URL: https://doi.org/10.24412/3162-2364-2022-86-2-22-
33

9 Ashrafyan, K. Junta and the laws of Valladolid of 1513
as a continuation of the Laws of Burgos of 1512. / K. E.
Ashrafyan // European Scientific Conference: collection of
articles of the XXV International Scientific and Practical
Conference, Penza, April 07, 2021. Penza: Science and
Education, 2021. pp. 66-72
Zenodo URL: https://doi.org/10.5281/zenodo.5288124

10 Ashrafyan, Konstantin. From the Encomienda of
Nicolas Ovando to the Laws of Burgos (1503–1512) //
Humanitarian Scientific Bulletin. V. 6. № 2021. pp. 1–10.
URL: https://doi.org/10.5281/zenodo.8420744

11 Ashrafyan, Konstantin. Encomienda as a system of
relations between Aborigines and settlers of the New
World through the prism of the policy of Christianization
and slavery (1492-1504) / // Humanitarian Scientific
Bulletin. V. 3. № 2021. pp. 8–16.
URL: https://doi.org/10.5281/zenodo.8420873

12 Ashrafyan, K. The policy of catholic monarchs and
Popes in the New World on the Christianization of the
population and the policy of local authorities (1492–1513)
// Samara journal of science. 2023. V. 10 (1). № 2021. pp.
230–236.
URL: https://snv63.ru/2309-4370/article/view/70368

DOI: 10.17816/snv2021101208
URL: https://doi.org/10.5281/zenodo.8421062

13 Ashrafyan, K. Images of Indians from Spanish Florida in the XVI century: truth and lies, speculation and facts. Zenodo, 2023.
URL: https://doi.org/10.5281/zenodo.8409846

14 Ashrafyan, K. Images of Indians from Spanish Florida in the XVI century: truth and lies, speculation and facts. Zenodo, 2023.
URL: https://doi.org/10.5281/zenodo.8409846

15 Ashrafyan, K. Interdisciplinary interaction in science on the example of considering the discovery and development of Florida in the XVI century // Modern problems of science and society. Monograph. Chapter 12. Penza,: MCNS «Nauka i prosveshcenie», 2021. pp. 145–161. ZENODO. DOI: 10.5281/zenodo.5324430
URL: https://doi.org/10.5281/zenodo.5324315

16 Ashrafyan, K. The Burgos Laws of 1512 as the progenitors of "human rights": the circumstances and necessity of their adoption and consequences (1512)// Humanitarian Scientific Bulletin2021. № 5. pp. 14–21 ZENODO URL: https://doi.org/10.5281/zenodo.4911300

17 Ashrafyan, Konstantin. Chapter 17. Translation of the text "memories" ("memoir") by Hernando de Escalante de Fontaneda into Russian: a story about the tribes of Florida in the mid-XVI century // Innovations in science, society, education. Monograph. Penza, Russia: MCNS "Nauka i Prosveshcenie", 2021. pp. 203–219.

ZENODO URL: https://doi.org/10.5281/zenodo.5411750

18 Ashrafyan, Konstantin. The lands of the Florida Indians in the middle of the xvi century: map of the leaders of Florida according to the memoirs of Hernando de Fontaneda // The best work 2021. Penza, Russia: MCNS «Nauka i Prosveshcenie», 2021. pp. 44–55.
ZENODO DOI: https://doi.org/10.5281/zenodo.5397321.

19 Ashrafyan, K. Information about the settlement and making of the aborigenes tribes on the Florida peninsula in the XVI century: a history of return from non-existence // The best scientific work of 2021: a collection of articles of the XXXII International Competition of scientific papers, which will be held on August 15, 2021 in Penza. MCNS «Nauka i Prosveshcenie», 2021. pp. 44–55.
ZENODO URL: https://doi.org/10.5281/zenodo.5396935

20 Ashrafyan K. The hypothesis of the inevitability of the failure of attempts to develop the south of the Florida peninsula from 1513 to 1525. // Science, education, society in the context of digitalization: monograph / edited by G. Y. Gulyaev ; International Centre for Scientific Cooperation "Science and Education". Penza, 2021. pp. 143-156. (Chapter 8).
MONOGRAPH M-152
URL: https://naukaip.ru/wp-content/uploads/2021/05/MOH-152.pdf
URL: https://www.elibrary.ru/item.asp?id=45734534

21 Ashrafyan, Konstantin. Chapter 11. The disappeared tribes of Florida as an urgent issue of modern science and

education: the need to get out of oblivion of knowledge about the history of American peoples of the "pre-seminol era" // Topical issues of modern science and education monograph. Penza, Russia: MCNS «Nauka i prosveshcenie», 2021. pp. 125–140.
ZENODO DOI: 10.5281/zenodo.5348362
ZENODO URL: https://doi.org/10.5281/zenodo.5356955

22 Ashrafyan, K. History, bioarchaeology, psychology, sociology of youth and law: the interaction of sciences during the consideration of meetings opening Florida in XVI // Collection of materials. Abstracts of the presentation at the conference: XIV Congress of Anthropologists and Ethnologists of Russia. Section 31. Tomsk. 6-9 July 2021. pp.404-405
URL:
https://www.researchgate.net/publication/353435401_IST
ORIA_BIOARHEOLOGIA_PSIHOLOGIA_POLITOLOG
IA_I_PRAVO_VZAIMODEJSTVIE_NAUK_PRI_RASS
MOTRENII_SOBYTIJ_OTKRYTIA_FLORIDY_V_XVI_
v
ZENODO URL: https://doi.org/10.5281/zenodo.8419448

23 Ashrafyan, K. The history of translations of the "Memoirs" and other texts by Fernando de Escalante Fontaneda: the history of translations, comments, and drawings to the text // Gumanitarny`j nauchny`j vestnik. 2021. T. 8. № 2021. pp. 1–7.
URL: https://doi.org/10.5281/zenodo.5503650
ZENODO URL: https://doi.org/10.5281/zenodo.8419413

24 Ashrafyan, K. Translation "requirements for indians" («requerimiento a los indios. 28 julio 1513»): preserving the past for the future // Science and education: the last, created by the future: a collection of articles XXXVI International Scientific and Practical Conference. : Zenodo, 2021. pp. 68–73.
URL: https://doi.org/10.5281/zenodo.5711857

25 Ashraf'yan, K. Translation into Russian language of three bulls from 1493 by pope alexander vi: bull no. 1 "breve inter caetera", bull no. 3 "Eximiae Devotionis" and bull no. 4 "Dudum Siquide". // Science, innovation, education: current issues and modern aspects. Monograph. Chapter 14. Penza: MCNS «Nauka i Prosveshcenie», 2021. pp. 195–213.
Change and new edition: 22 05 2022
ZENODO DOI: 10.5281/zenodo.6570349

26 Ashrafyan, K. Two views at the "Fountain of Youth" as the main reason for organizing an expedition to discover new lands in the first quarter of the XVI century. // Science, innovation, society in modern conditions. Monograph. Penza: MCNS «Nauka i Prosveshhenie», 2022. pp. 122–135. (Chapter 11)
ZENODO URL: https://doi.org/10.5281/zenodo.6924090

27 Ashrafyan, K. Problem points of various research methods and prospects for their solution in the study of Spanish Florida of the XVI-XVIII centuries // "Revista Transilvania" January. 2022. T. 4. № 2022. pp. 86–96.
SCOPUS Q-1

URL: https://revistatransilvania.ro/problem-points-of-various-research-methods-and-prospects-for-their-solution-in-the-study-of-16th-to-18th-century-spanish-florida/.
URL: https://doi.org/10.51391/trva.2022.04.10.

28 Ashrafyan, K. Spaniards in Montenegro: the failure of the last crusade of the "Holy League" or the secret of the fortress "Španjola" in Herceg-Novi// Sciences of Europe. 2022. V. 2. № 86. pp. 22–33.
URL: https://www.europe-science.com/wp-content/uploads/2022/01/Sciences-of-Europe-No-86-2022-Vol.-2.pdf

29 Ashraf'yan, K. E. Substitution of cultures: the history of the disappeared culture of the Indians of South Florida and Indians in the perception of the modern man in the post-Soviet space // Researcher: Collection of scientific articles and conference materials dedicated to the centenary and birthday Yu.M. Lotmana, Moskva, 14 May 2022. Moskva "Sputnik+", 2022. pp. 4-17.
ZENODO URL: https://doi.org/10.5281/zenodo.6946080

30 Ashrafyan, K. "Problems of Interdisciplinary Research in considering the Discovery and Development of Spanish Florida in the 16th Century." Zenodo, 2021. English version of 42nd International Competition of Scientific Works (16 July 2021). Chapter 12. Penza: MCNS «Nauka i Prosveshcenie», 2021.
DOI: 10.5281/zenodo.5276539.
ZENODO URL: https://zenodo.org/records/5276539

31 Ashrafyan, K.E. Additions and clarifications in the Russian translations of the 1493 bull of pope alexander vi:

bull no. 1 "breves inter caetera", and bull no. 4 "Dudum Siquide"// Annali d\'Italiaю Historical Sciences. 2022. T. 33. № 2022. pp. 106–115.
URL: https://www.anditalia.com/wp-content/uploads/2022/07/Annali-d'Italia-№33-2022.pdf

32 Ashrafyan K., Peña Àngel Pascual. Understanding the place of Catalonia and Catalans in world history in the light of historical cause-and-effect relationships in the light of the confrontation between the Christian and Muslim worlds // The Scientific Heritage. 2022. №98. pp. 17-26
URL: http://www.scientific-heritage.com/wp-content/uploads/2022/10/The-scientific-heritage-No-98-98-2022.pdf
URL: https://cyberleninka.ru/article/n/understanding-the-place-of-catalonia-and-catalans-in-world-history-in-the-light-of-historical-cause-and-effect-relationships-in-the/viewer
ZENODO URL: https://zenodo.org/records/7144159

33 Ashrafyan, K. E. Questions that arise during the study "great discoveries" and nuances of the occurrence of some conflicts in the New World// Science, society, education in modern conditions. Monograph. Chapter 20. Penza: MCNS «Nauka i Prosveshcenie», 2022. pp. 243–259.
URL: https://doi.org/10.5281/zenodo.7212711

34 Ashrafyan, K. E. Questions that arise during the study "great discoveries" and nuances of the occurrence of some conflicts in the New World// Science, society, education in modern conditions. Monograph. Chapter 20. Penza: MCNS «Nauka i Prosveshcenie», 2022. pp. 243–259.
ZENODO URL: https://doi.org/10.5281/zenodo.7212711

35 Ashrafyan, K. E. Periodization of the discovery and development of Florida in the 16th century in the light of answers to questions of modern science and education // current issues of modern science and education. Monograph. Chapter 9. Penza: MCNS «Nauka i Prosveshcenie», 2023. pp. 108–121.
ZENODO URL: https://doi.org/10.5281/zenodo.8417567

36 Ashrafyan, K. E. The chronology of the discovery and development of Florida in the 16th century. Part 1: Introduction to the chronology of the discovery, development, and Christianisation of Florida in the 16thcentury. In: Bulletin of Moscow Region State University. Series: History and Political Sciences, 2023, no. 2, pp. 86–98.
DOI: 10.18384/2310-676X-2023-2-86-98
URL:
https://www.istpolitmgou.ru/jour/article/view/1633/1485
 https://doi.org/10.18384/2310-676X-2023-2-86-98

37 Ashrafyan K. E. The chronology of the discovery and development of Florida in the 16th century Part 2: The first stage of the discovery and development of Florida from 1513 to 1516 in: Bulletin of Moscow Region State University. Series: History and Political Sciences, 2023, no. 2, pp. 65–78
DOI: 10 18384/2310-676x-2023-3-65-78.
URL:
https://www.istpolitmgou.ru/jour/article/view/1673/1497

38 Ashrafyan, K. About the question of the ownership of the land of the Atlantic coast of North America "de jure" from 1494 to 1525 and the study of its "de facto" by Portugal and England at the end of the XIV century – the beginning of the XV century // MODERN SCIENCE: CURRENT ISSUES, ACHIEVEMENTS AND INNOVATIONS. Penza: MCNS «Nauka i Prosveshcenie»", 2023. pp. 118–134. (Chapter 10) ZENODO URL: https://doi.org/10.5281/zenodo.8313226

39 Ashrafyan, K. The full translation into Russian of the "Cèllere codex" - document by Janus Verazanus on the expedition of 1524. // Modern Science:
current events, achievements, and innovations. Monograph. MCNS «Nauka i Prosveshcenie». 2023. pp. 135-160. (Chapter 11).
DOI: 10.5281/zenodo.8310238
ZENODO URL: https://doi.org/10.5281/zenodo.8310238

40 Ashrafyan K. E. The chronology of the discovery and development of Florida in the 16th century. Part 3: The second stage of the discovery and development of Florida from 1516 to 1520. In: Bulletin of State University of Education. Series: History and Political Sciences, 2023, no. 4, pp. 53–69.
DOI: 10.18384/2949-5164-2023-4-53-69.
URL:
https://www.istpolitmgou.ru/jour/article/view/1725/1510

41 Ashrafyan K. E. Chronology of the discovery and development of Florida in the 16 th century Part 4: The third stage of the discovery and development of Florida (The beginning of the reign of Emperor Charles V and the

continuation of the exploration of Florida 1520–1522) in: Bulletin of Federal State University of Education. Series: History and Political Sciences, 2024, no. 1, pp. 108–122
DOI: 10 18384/2949-5164-2024-1-108-122
URL:
https://www.istpolitmgou.ru/jour/article/view/1815/1548

42 Ashrafyan, Konstantin. (2022). Spanish colonization of Florida in the first quarter of the 16th century: methods, features, causes of failure (English version) // [Zenodo].
THESIS URL:
https://ia902608.us.archive.org/16/items/ashrafyan-thesis-konstantin.-thesis.-enlish-language.-2022/ASHRAFYAN%20THESIS%20Konstantin.%20Thesis.%20Enlish%20language.%202022.pdf
 THESIS ZENODO URL:
https://doi.org/10.5281/zenodo.7452063.

43 Ashrafyan K. E. The chronology of the discovery and development of Florida in the 16th century Part 2: The first stage of the discovery and development of Florida from 1513 to 1516 in: Bulletin of Moscow Region State University. Series: History and Political Sciences, 2023, no 2, pp. 65–78
DOI: 10 18384/2310-676x-2023-3-65-78.
URL:
https://www.istpolitmgou.ru/jour/article/view/1673/1497
 DOI: https://doi.org/10.18384/2310-676X-2023-3-65-78

44 Ashrafyan, K. E. About the question of the belonging of the land of the Atlantic coast of North America "de jure" from 1494 to 1525 and the study of its "de facto" Portugal and England at the end of the XIV century – the beginning

of the XV century. [Electronic resource] /K. E. Ashrafyan // Modern science: current issues, achievements, and innovation.2023. C. 118–134. (Chapter 10). 2023. pp. 118-134.
ZENONO URL: https://zenodo.org/records/8313226.
URL: https://naukaip.ru/wp-content/uploads/2023/08/MOH-201-1.pdf
(Monogpraph MOH-201. Part 11).

45 Ashrafyan K. E. The chronology of the discovery and development of Florida in the 16th century. Part 3: The second stage of the discovery and development of Florida from 1516 to 1520. In: Bulletin of State University of Education. Series: History and Political Sciences, 2023, no. 4, pp. 53–69.
DOI: 10.18384/2949-5164-2023-4-53-69
URL:
https://www.istpolitmgou.ru/jour/article/view/1725/1510
https://doi.org/10.18384/2949-5164-2023-4-53-69.
ZENODO DOI: 10.5281/zenodo.10429479

46 Ashrafyan K. E. Chronology of the discovery and development of Florida in the 16th century Part 4: The third stage of the discovery and development of Florida (The beginning of the reign of Emperor Charles V and the continuation of the exploration of Florida 1520–1522) in: Bulletin of Federal State University of Education. Series: History and Political Sciences, 2024, no. 1, pp. 108–122
DOI: 10 18384/2949-5164-2024-1-108-122
URL:
https://www.istpolitmgou.ru/jour/article/view/1815/1548

BOOKS

47 History of Florida by ... = Historia de Florida por…
/Konstantin Ashrafyan. - [S. l.] : [s. n.], 2019-.Book 1:
Blood and Cheating. 1511 = Sangre y Mentiras. 1511. -
2019. - 236 p. : ill.; B07W78P1TB
https://www.amazon.com/Historia-Florida-por-Libro-
Ingles-
ebook/dp/B07W78P1TB/ref=monarch_sidesheet_title

48 Ashrafyan, K. History of Florida by… Myths and
Heroes. 1511-1513 / K. Ashrafyan. — 1st ed. —
Charleston : Create Space Publisher, 2016. — Vol. 2. —
332 p. — History of Florida by…. — ISBN 978-
1541342743. — URL:
https://dlib.rsl.ru/viewer/01008906119#?page=1.

49 Ashrafyan, K. History of Florida by… Fountain of
Youth 1513-1514 / K. Ashrafyan. — 1st ed. —
Charleston: Create Space Publisher, 2016. — Vol. 3. —
325 c. — History of Florida by…. — ISBN 978-
1542459525. — URL:
https://dlib.rsl.ru/viewer/01010060957#?page=2

50 History of Florida by ... = Historia de Florida por… /
Konstantin Ashrafyan. - [S. l.] : [s. n.], 2012-.Book 4 Part
1: The mystery of the maps of Christopher Columbus.
Spain-Turkey 1513 – 1514 = Mapas de rompecabezas de
Cristóbal Colón. España - Turquía 1513-1514. 2016. - 330
p.; ISBN 978-1987687002
URL:
https://viewer.rsl.ru/ru/rsl01010060991?page=1&rotate=0
&theme=white

51 History of Florida by ... = Historia de Florida por... / Konstantin Ashrafyan. - [S. l.] : [s. n.], 2012-.Book 4 Part 2: The mystery of the maps of Christopher Columbus. Spain-Turkey-Vatican-Rhodes-Florida. 1513 - 1514 = El misterio de los mapas de Cristóbal Colón. España-Turquía-Vaticano-Rodas-Florida. 1513-1514. - cop. 2016. - 292 p. : ill.; ISBN 978-1720837299
URL: https://dlib.rsl.ru/viewer/01010061027#?page=1

52 Ashrafyan, K. Spanish colonization of Florida in the first quarter XVI century: methods, features, reasons of failures. Amazon Italia. Torrazza. Piermonte. 2024. 329 p. ISBN 979-887-685-348-6
https://viewer.rsl.ru/ru/rsl01012867667?page=1&rotate=0&theme=white
https://www.amazon.com/s?k=Spanish+colonization+of+Florida+in+the+first+quarter+XVI+century&i=digital-text&crid=L3BHUYW7D8R9&sprefix=spanish+colonization+of+florida+in+the+first+quarter+xvi+century%2Cdigital-text%2C807&ref=nb_sb_noss

53 Ashrafyan, K. E. Katon : the historical novel about ancient Rome / Ashrafyan K. E. ; [artist: Ashrafyan Konstantin et al.]. - [B. M.]: B.I.], 2004. - 443, [1] p. : ill . ; 22 . - 1000 copies - ISBN 5-85597-030-2.
URL:
https://viewer.rsl.ru/ru/rsl01007895163?page=1&rotate=0&theme=white

The contact of author:
e-mail: *kea6465@gmail.com*
Ashrafyan Konstantin (PhD of Historical Sciences)

Social
piramid
of Calusa tribe
(create by
Dr. Ashrafyan K.)

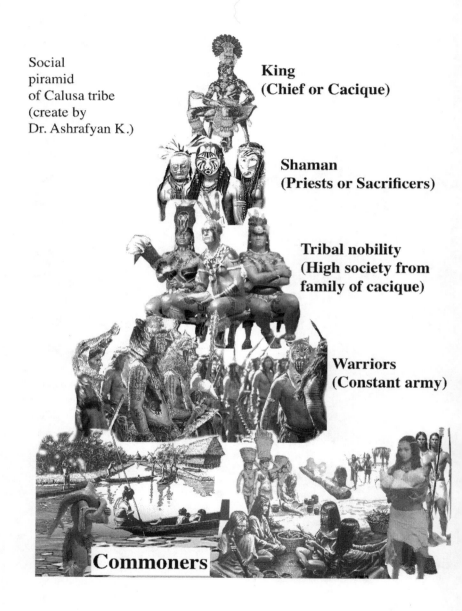

**King
(Chief or Cacique)**

**Shaman
(Priests or Sacrificers)**

**Tribal nobility
(High society from
family of cacique)**

**Warriors
(Constant army)**

Commoners